Frontispiece.

POEMS WRITTEN FOR
A CHILD

By TWO FRIENDS

Anchora Spei

STRAHAN AND CO., PUBLISHERS

56 LUDGATE HILL, LONDON

1868

CONTENTS.

—◆—

FAIRY FACTS.

CROWNS FOR CHILDREN.

The children crown'd themselves with roses,
   And all the roses died !
Pale on the soft brown locks they lay,
Like a dream of spring on a cold white day,
   In the barren winter-tide.
      Oh, throw the fading vision by !
      Make a crown that cannot die.

The children crown'd themselves with diamonds,
   And could not bear the weight ;
Down they droop their weary curls,
Like a leaf that falls or a sail that furls,
   When the night is dark and late.
      Oh, throw away the useless things !
      Crowns should be as light as wings.

The children crown'd themselves with wishes,
   And every wish came true ;
Love lies soft on each fair head,
Kisses dry the tears they shed,—
   Hope each day is new.
      Keep that crown, nor keep in vain !
      If it dies, it grows again.

                B.

A NORTH POLE STORY.

A FACT.

Up where the world grows cold,
    Under the sharp North star,
The wrinkled ice is very old,
    And the life of man is far;
None to see when the fog falls white,
    And none to shiver and hear
How wild the bears are in the night,
    Which lasts for half a year!

B

The wind may blow as it will,
  But it cannot shake a tree,
Nor stir the waves which lie so still
  On the corpse of that dead sea!
The sun comes out over flowerless strands
  Where only ice-tears flow,
When the North weeps for sweet wood-
    lands
  Which she must never know.

Earth speaks with awful lips,
  No place for man is here!
Between my bergs I'll crush your
    ships,
  If you will come too near;
You shall be slain by bitter wind,
  Or starved on barren shore,

My cruel snow shall strike you blind;
　Go,—trouble me no more!"

But British men are fain
　To venture on and through,
And when you tell them to refrain,
　They set themselves to do;
Into the secrets of the snow
　They hurry and they press,
And answer Nature's coldest "No"
　With a great shout of "Yes."

It was a little band
　Went on that dangerous track,
To do a message from our land,
　And to bring an answer back;
The frost had bound their good ship tight,
　And years were come and gone,

When a few brave hearts, as best they
    might,
  Went over the shores alone.

And as one strode so bold,
  He saw a sight of fear,—
Nine white wolves came over the wold,
  And they were watching a deer;
By three and by two and by one
  A cunning half-moon they made,
They glanced at each other and did not
    run,
  But crept like creatures afraid.

They knew what they were about,
  And the poor thing knew it too,
 tIturned its head like a child in doubt,
  And shrank, and backward drew;

But whether it look'd to left or right
  It met a savage eye,   [sight,
And the man stood still and saw the
  And felt that it must die.

Backward, trembling and fast,
  And onward, crafty and slow,
And over the cliff's sheer edge at last,
  And crash on the ice below;
But then with a whirl and a plunge and
     a whoop,
  The wolves are down the hill;
They break their ranks, that wild white
     troop,
  When it is time to kill.

And days and nights went past,
  And the men grew weary and pale,

Scanty food and freezing blast,
  And hearts beginning to fail!
The wanderer knew his steps were slow,
  And his eyes were languid and dim,
When nine white wolves came over the
    snow,
  And they were watching—him.

He saw them gather and glance,
  And he remember'd the deer!
He saw them frame their cunning ad-
    vance,
  And he felt a little fear!
But never a hair's breadth did he swerve,
  Nor lower his looks a whit,
He faced the cruel scimetar-curve,
  And then walked up to it!

There is never a beast so strong
  As to bear a brave man's eye!
They crouch'd; they look'd as if no-
    thing was wrong,
  And then they turn'd to fly.
The man stood still and drew his
    breath,
  When he saw the scattering ranks;
He had been face to face with
    death:
  I hope he utter'd thanks.

There's a fireside far away
  A little anxious now,
Where a man shall sit one joyful
    day,
  And tell of the world of snow;

And tell of the wolves who sup so
    grim,
  And leave no bone behind;
And how they meant to sup on him,
  But look'd, and changed their mind!

Page 9

SONG.

O Moon—said the children—O Moon,
    that shineth fair,
Why do you stay so far away, so high
    above us there?
O Moon, you must be very cold from
    shining on the sea;
If you would come and play with us,
    how happy we should be!

O children—said the Moon—I shine
    above your head,
That I may light the ships at night
    when the sun has gone to bed;
That I may show the beggar-boy his
    way across the moor,
And bring the busy farmer home to his
    own cottage-door.

O Moon—said the children—may we
    shine in your place?
They say that I have sunny hair, and I
    a sparkling face.
To light the ships and beggar-boys we
    greatly do desire;
And you might come and warm your-
    self before the nurs'ry fire!

O children—said the Moon—we have
    each allotted parts:
'Tis yours to shine by love divine on
    happy human hearts;
'Tis mine to make the pathway bright
    of wanderers that roam;
'Tis yours to scatter endless light on
    those that stay at home!

LITTLE PAT AND THE PARSON.

HE stands at the door of the church
    peeping in,
  No troublesome beadle is near him;
The preacher is talking of sinners and
      sin,
  And little Pat trembles to hear him;
A poor little fellow alone and forlorn,
  Who never knew parent or duty,—

His head is uncover'd, his jacket is torn,
  And hunger has wither'd his beauty.

The white-headed gentleman shut in
    the box
  Seems growing more angry each
    minute,—
He doubles his fist, and the cushion he
    knocks,
  As if anxious to know what is in it.
He scolds at the people who sit in the
    pews,—
  Pat takes them for kings and prin-
    cesses.
(With his little bare feet—he delights
    in their shoes:
  In his rags—he feels proud of their
    dresses!)

The Parson exhorts them to think of
    their need,
  To turn from the world's dissipation,
The naked to clothe and the hungry to
    feed,—
  Pat listens with strong approbation !
And when the old clergyman walks
    down the aisle,
  Pat runs up to meet him right gladly,
" Shure, give me my dinner," says he
    with a smile,
   " And a jacket,—I want them quite
    badly !"

The kings and princesses indignantly
    stare,
  The beadle gets word of the danger,

And, shaking his silver-tipp'd stick in
    the air,
  Looks knives at the poor little stranger.
But Pat's not afraid, he is sparkling
    with joy,
  And cries—who so willing to cry it?—
"You'll give me my dinner—I'm *such*
    a poor boy:
  You said so—now *don't* you deny it!"

The pompous old beadle may grumble
    and glare,
  And growl about robbers and arson;
But the boy who has faith in the ser-
    mon stands there,
  And smiles at the white-headed Par-
    son!

The kings and princesses may wonder
and frown,
 And whisper he wants better teach-
ing;
But the white-headed Parson looks ten-
derly down
 On the boy who has faith in his
preaching.

He takes him away without question or
blame,
 As eager as Patsy to press on,
For he thinks a good dinner (and Pat
thinks the same)
 Is the moral that lies in the lesson.
And after long years, when Pat, hand-
somely drest—

A smart footman—is asked to deter-
    mine
Of all earthly things what's the thing
    he likes best,
    He says, " Och! shure, the master's
    ould sermin!"

WOODEN LEGS.

Two children sat in the twilight,
  Murmuring soft and low;
Said one, " I'll be a sailor-lad,
  With my boat ahoy! yo ho!
For sailors are most loved of all
  In every happy home,
And tears of grief or gladness fall
  Just as they go or come."

But the other child said sadly,
  " Ah, do not go to sea,
Or in the dreary winter nights
  What will become of me ?
For if the wind began to blow,
  Or thunder shook the sky,
Whilst you were in your boat, yo ho !
  What could I do but cry ?"

Then he said, " I'll be a soldier,
  With a delightful gun,
And I'll come home with a wooden leg,
  As heroes have often done."
She screams at that, and prays and begs,
  While tears—half anger—start,
" Don't talk about your wooden legs,
  Unless you'd break my heart !"

He answer'd her rather proudly,
   If so, what *can* I be,
If I must not have a wooden leg
   And must not go to sea?   [night,
How could the Queen sleep sound at
   Safe from the scum and dregs,
If English boys refused to fight
   For fear of wooden legs?"

She hung her head repenting,
   And trying to be good,
But her little hand stroked tenderly
   The leg of flesh and blood!
And with her rosy mouth she kiss'd
   The knickerbocker'd knee,
And sigh'd, " Perhaps—if you insist—
   You'd *better* go to sea!"

Then he flung his arms about her,
  And laughingly he spoke,
" But I've seen many honest tars
  With legs of British oak!
Oh, darling! when I am a man,
  With beard of shining black,
I'll be a *hero* if I can,
  And you must not hold me back."

She kiss'd him as she answer'd,
  I'll try what I can do,—
And Wellington had *both* his legs,
  And Cœur de Lion too!
And Garibaldi," here she sighed,
  I know *he's* lame—but there—
He's *such* a hero—none beside
  Like *him* could do and dare!"

So the children talk'd in the twilight
  Of many a setting sun,
And she'd stroke his chin and clap her
    hands
  That the beard had not begun ;
For though she meant to be brave and
    good
  When he play'd a hero's part,
Yet often the thought of the leg of wood
  Lay heavy on her heart !

NELLY'S SHILLING.

O'ER the soft green meadow-lands
   Little Nelly trips along,
With a basket in her hands
   And upon her lips a song,—
Singing, " Buy my watercresses,
   Watercresses, great and small;
Mother in such deep distress is,
   If I do not sell them all!"

With her little naked feet
   Glancing out upon the stones,
Through the town's frequented street,
   On she runs, nor hardship owns;
Singing, " Buy the watercresses,
   I have search'd for high and low,
Won't you kindly buy them ? 'Yes' is
   Far the nicest word I know !"

Something lies upon the ground,
   How she turns it o'er and o'er;
It is white and bright and round,
   Sure she's seen the thing before !
Yes it is—it *is* a shilling !
   Did it tumble from the sky ?
Up she looks, extremely willing
   To catch more if floating by !

Dear shop-window! oft on thee
   She has turn'd her hungry eyes;
Now a purchaser is she,
   To select and criticize!
But the dainty dishes in it
   Do her little brain confuse,
For a shilling has *no* limit,
   There is *nothing* she can't choose!

For the common loaf of bread
   Her contempt is unsupprest;
" Beef is very good," she said,
   " But perhaps it is not *best;*
Ham there is not any harm in,
   Currants look divine in rice,
Sausages are really charming,
   And plum-pudding is too nice!"

Then a dreadful thought arose,
　　And her little heart stood still.
Is it mine?   Ah, no one knows!
　　Shall I keep it?   Yes, I will!
Yet reluctantly she lingers
　　At the window she loves best,
With the shilling in her fingers
　　And distraction in her breast!

Suddenly with eager start,
　　Like a hunted thing she flies,
Clasps the shilling to her heart,
　　Breathless, panting, onward hies;
Through a noble street she ventures,
　　What can she be doing there?
By an open doorway enters,
　　'Tis the mansion of the MAYOR!

Watercresses she has sold
   At that door in humble awe,
And the creature has been told
   He is CHIEF MAN of the LAW!
So she seeks him trembling, shaking,
   Finds him cheerful, calm, and free,
And, her small heart almost breaking,
   Lays her shilling on his knee!

Then the good man heard her speak
   (Though her words were wild and few),
Stroked her hair, and kiss'd her cheek,
   Told her she was brave and true;
With importance took the shilling,
   Said it was a stray and waif,
And the law was bound and willing
   To protect and keep it safe.

And a guinea made of gold
  Placed in her astonish'd hand,
Such a sum she scarce can hold—
  Such a sum scarce understand;
Nell, in her triumphant glory,
  Holds her guinea by the rim;
But the good man counts her story
  As a richer gain for him!

THE WIVES OF BRIXHAM.

A TRUE STORY.

You see the gentle water,
　　How silently it floats;
How cautiously, how steadily,
　　It moves the sleepy boats;
And all the little loops of pearl
　　It strews along the sand,
Steal out as leisurely as leaves
　　When summer is at hand.

But you know it can be angry,
    And thunder from its rest,
When the stormy taunts of winter
    Are flying at its breast;
And if you like to listen,
    And draw your chairs around,
I'll tell you what it did one night
    When you were sleeping sound.

The merry boats of Brixham
    Go out to search the seas;
A staunch and sturdy fleet are they,
    Who love a swinging breeze;
And before the woods of Devon,
    And the silver cliffs of Wales,   [fall,
You may see, when summer evenings
    The light upon their sails.

But when the year grows darker,
   And grey winds hunt the foam,
They go back to Little Brixham,
   And ply their toil at home.
And thus it chanced one winter's night,
   When a storm began to roar,
That all the men were out at sea,
   And all the wives on shore.

Then as the wind grew fiercer,
   The women's cheeks grew white,—
It was fiercer in the twilight,
   And fiercest in the night;
The strong clouds set themselves like ice
   Without a star to melt,
The blackness of the darkness
   Was darkness to be felt.

The storm, like an assassin,
   Went on its wicked way,
And struck a hundred boats adrift,
   To reel about the bay.   [men!
They meet, they crash—God keep the
   God give a moment's light!
There is nothing but the tumult,
   And the tempest, and the night.

The men on shore were anxious,—
   They dreaded what they knew;
What do you think the women did?
   Love taught them what to do!
Outspake a wife, "We've beds at home,
   We'll burn them for a light,—
Give us the men and the bare ground!
   We want no more to-night."

They took the grandame's blanket,
  Who shiver'd and bade them go;
They took the baby's pillow,
  Who could not say them no;
And they heap'd a great fire on the pier;
  And knew not all the while
If they were heaping a bonfire,
  Or only a funeral pile.

And, fed with precious food, the flame
  Shone bravely on the black,
Till a cry rang through the people,
  "A boat is coming back!"
Staggering dimly through the fog,
  Come shapes of fear and doubt;
But when the first prow strikes the pier,
  Cannot you hear them shout?

D

Then all along the breadth of flame
    Dark figures shriek'd and ran,
With, "Child, here comes your father!"
    Or, "Wife, is this your man?"
And faint feet touch the welcome stone,
    And wait a little while;
And kisses drop from frozen lips,
    Too tired to speak or smile.

So, one by one, they struggled in,
    All that the sea would spare;
We will not reckon through our tears
    The names that were not there;
But some went home without a bed,
    When all the tale was told,
Who were too cold with sorrow
    To know the night was cold.

And this is what the men must do
    Who work in wind and foam;
And this is what the women bear
    Who watch for them at home.
So when you see a Brixham boat
    Go out to face the gales,
Think of the love that travels
    Like light upon her sails!

HUNTING THE WIND.

WHEN the fire is burning bright,
  And the kettle hums and sings
In the happy winter night,
  Children talk of many things:
Talk of mermaids in the sea,
  And of fairies in the wood,
Pretty things that ought to be,
  And surely would be if they could!

Then the wind comes creeping near,
  Tired of fighting with the trees,
List'ning with a sort of fear
  To such merry sounds as these;
Crying like a child in pain,
  With a foolish ceaseless din,
Knocking on the glass again,
  Begging them to let it in!

Outspake little Curlyhead,
  "This poor wind is taken ill;
Soon it will be lying dead
  On the frozen window-sill.
Very cruel children we
  If we let it die alone,—
If we do not run and see
  Why it makes that dreary moan."

And he flung the window wide,
    And the wind came tearing through,
Dashing everything aside
    With its hulla-bulla-loo!
Blowing both the candles out,
    Roaring, rushing, raving by,
Scattering the smoke about,
    While the children scream and fly!

Outspake little Curlyhead,
    Though his breath he scarce can draw,
"Nurse would snatch us off to bed
    If this horrid mess she saw!
Hunt the thankless creature low,—
    Seize it, catch it, if you can.
I will teach it manners, though,
    If I live to be a man!"

Chubby arms are flung about,
  Toddling feet run here and there,—
Some would chase the creature out,
  Some would tie it to a chair;
While the eldest of the crowd
  Shuts the window where she stands,
Little Blue-eyes shouts aloud,
  She has caught it in her hands!

Curlyhead, with manly rage,
  Stamps his foot and cries " Hurrah!"
Red-cheeks brings an empty cage,
  Where no pretty birdies are;
Little Blue-eyes, fat and fair,
  Hollow'd hands above her head,
Moves with cautious footsteps where
  Red-cheeks stands with Curlyhead.

Curlyhead the cage doth hold,
   Red-cheeks keeps it open wide;
Little Blue-eyes, when she's told,
   Thrusts her two fat hands inside.
Ah! they have the fellow now,
   Little Blue-eyes shouts anew;
Curlyhead performs a bow,
   Red-cheeks makes a curtsey too!

Hang the cage up, if you will,
   Clap your hands, ye hunters rare.
But he is so sad and still,
   Are you *sure* that he is there?
Ah! the days are coming when
   You'll have many a chase as blind;
Capture, triumph, laugh, and then
   But an empty casket find!

THE SINGING LESSON.

A NIGHTINGALE made a mistake!
   She sang a few notes out of tune,
Her heart was ready to break,
   And she hid from the moon!
She wrung her claws, poor thing,
   But was far too proud to speak,
So tuck'd her head under her wing,
   And pretended to be asleep!

A lark, arm-in-arm with a thrush,
   Came sauntering up to the place;
The nightingale felt herself blush,
   Though feathers hid her face;
She knew they had heard her song,
   She *felt* them snigger and sneer,
She thought that this life was too long,
   And wish'd she could skip a year!

"O nightingale!" coo'd a dove;
   "O nightingale! what's the use?
You bird of beauty and love,
   Why behave like a goose?
Don't skulk away from our sight
   Like common contemptible fowl;
You bird of joy and delight,
   Why behave like an owl?

Only think of all you have done,
　　Only think of all you *can do;*
A false note is really fun
　　From such a bird as you!
Lift up your proud little crest,
　　Open your musical beak;
Other birds have to do their best,
　　You need only *speak.*"

The nightingale shyly took
　　Her head from under her wing,
And giving the dove a look,
　　Straightway began to sing.
There was never a bird could pass,
　　The night was divinely calm,
And the people stood on the grass
　　To hear that wonderful psalm!

The nightingale did not care,
   She only sang to the skies;
Her song ascended there,
   And there she fix'd her eyes.
The people that stood below
   She knew but little about;
And this story's a moral, I know,
   If you'll try to find it out!

A CHILD'S THOUGHT.

LITTLE beggar children, with your little
    ragged dresses,
Does love atone for joys unknown by
    beautiful caresses?
Or, do you live in happy homes as dear,
    perhaps, as this is,
And do you know that, come or go,
    you'll meet with eager kisses?

I often see you wandering, and wonder
        just as often,
If love makes bright your homes at
        night, your misery to soften;
And do you ever, *ever* play, you help-
    less little creatures?
And can you spell and read as well?
        And have you any teachers?

If I was kept so dirty, I should think
        that nothing matters;
I never could feel very good in rags and
        tears and tatters.
And if I'd not one bit of food, and saw
        a lovely dinner,
I almost feel that I could steal, and be
        a wicked sinner!

Little beggar children, my life is very
     pleasant,
The past is dear, the future clear, and,
     best of all, the present;
I am a happy little child, with love and
     joy about me,
And many a one would lose the sun,
     rather than live without me.

I think my feelings towards you should
     be so soft and tender,
And even I might plan, and try some
     tiny aid to render;
I'll often give you all I can out of my
     little treasure,
And I will pray—yes, every day—that
     you may have some pleasure!

A CHILD TO A ROSE.

WHITE Rose, talk to me!
  I don't know what to do.
Why do you say no word to me,
  Who say so much to you?
I'm bringing you a little rain,
  And I shall be so proud
If, when you feel it on your face,
  You take me for a cloud.

Here I come so softly,
  You cannot hear me walking;
If I take you by surprise,
  I may catch you talking.

Tell all your thoughts to me,
  Whisper in my ear;
Talk against the winter,
  He shall never hear.
I can keep a secret
  Since I was five years old.
Tell if you were frighten'd
  When first you felt the cold;
And, in the splendid summer,
  While you flush and grow,
Are you ever out of heart
  Thinking of the snow?

E

Did it feel like dying
　　When first your blossoms fell?
Did you know about the spring?
　　Did the daisies tell?
If you had no notion,
　　Only fear and doubt,
How I should have liked to see
　　When you found it out!
Such a beautiful surprise!
　　What must you have felt,
When your heart began to stir,
　　As the snow began to melt!

Do you mind the darkness
　　As I used to do?
You are not as old as I:
　　I can comfort you.

The little noises that you hear
  Are winds that come and go.
The world is always kind and safe,
  Whether you see or no;
And if you think that there are eyes
  About you near and far,
Perhaps the fairies are watching,—
  I know the angels are.

I think you must be lonely
  When all the colours fail,
And moonlight makes the garden
  So massy and so pale;
And *any*thing might come at last
  Out of those heaps of shade.
I would stay beside you
  If I were not afraid!

Children have no right to go
  Abroad in night and gloom;
But you are as safe in the garden
  As I am in my room.

White Rose, are you tired
  Of staying in one place?
Do you ever wish to see
  The wild-flowers face to face?
Do you know the woodbines,
  And the big, brown-crested reeds?
Do you wonder how they live
  So friendly with the weeds?
Have you any work to do
  When you've finish'd growing?
Shall you teach your little buds
  Pretty ways of blowing?

Do you ever go to sleep?
  Once I woke by night
And look'd out of the window,
  And there you stood, moon-white—
Moon-white in a mist of darkness,
  With never a word to say;
But you seem'd to move a little,
  And then I ran away.
I should have felt no wonder
  After I hid my head,
If I had found you standing
  Moon-white beside my bed.

White Rose, do you love me?
  I only wish you'd say.
I would work hard to please you
  If I but knew the way.

It seems so hard to be loving,
    And not a sign to see
But the silence and the sweetness
    For all as well as me.
I think you nearly perfect,
    In spite of all your scorns;
But, White Rose, if I were you,
    I *wouldn't* have those thorns!

JACK AND NED.

WHEN the ship is but a speck
　　To the landsman's feeble eye,
Sailors, lying on the deck,
　　Feel at home with sea and sky:
When the land's no longer seen
　　Light of heart the sailor is ;
Nothing sea and sky between
　　But that gallant ship of his !

Pretty Jack, with curly hair,
    Sunny eye and saucy lip,
Heart to love and soul to dare,
    Is the darling of the ship!
Mother's pet at mother's knee
    Only yesterday, it seems—
Now a sailor-boy is he,
    Mother sees him but in dreams!

Such a dashing little rogue!
    Such a loving little coax!
With a tiny touch of brogue
    To enhance his funny jokes;
With his childhood's innocence,
    And the colour of the skies
And a charming impudence
    Lighting his audacious eyes!

Jack is ailing—all deplore !
   Jack is ill—and joy has fled ;
Jack is dying—ah, no more !
   Yes, alas ! for—Jack is *dead !*
Grey old heads hang down in grief,
   O'er rough cheeks tears trickle fast ;
Strapping oaths give no relief—
   So they turn to prayer at last.

Then an aged seaman said,
   " Let me die instead of him ;
Take a worn-out craft instead
   Of a wherry tight and trim :
All my spars are getting loose—
   Ropes and rigging are not taut ;
Ned is useless, Jack's of use—
   Give the thing a moment's thought !"

Is Jack only in a faint
　　That his blue eyes open wide
At this rough-and-ready saint
　　Who, to save him, would have died?
In amazement all start back;
　　How they look and listen too—
" Ned, don't die," says little Jack;
　　" Who'll masthead me, if you do?"

So both lived to play their parts;
　　Death retreated from them far:
Sailors have such tender hearts
　　And such simple creatures are!
And I doubt, when all is said,
　　Which shows best in white and black,
An old sailor like our Ned
　　Or a sailor-boy like Jack!

In a cottage that I know
  Both are welcome as the sun ;
One, because it must be so—
  T'other for the sake of one :
In the mother's heart and home
  Ned may to the best aspire—
I have often seen him come
  To his corner by the fire.

If you ask the truth of Jack—
  Did he faint, or was he dead ?
Was his little soul brought back
  By the earnest prayer of Ned ?
What can tell us ?—who can say ?
  Answer none this earth may give :
We but know that Ned did pray—
  We but know that Jack did live !

STARS.

How pretty is each little star,
   Each tiny twinkler, soft and meek !
Yet many in this world there are
   Who do not know that stars can
     speak.

To them the skies are meaningless,
   A star is not a living thing;
They cannot hear the messages
   Those shining creatures love to bring.

Hush! listen! ah! it will not do;
    You do but listen with your ears;
And stars are understood by few,
    For it must be the heart that hears.

Look up, not *only* with your eyes;
    Ah! do you hear a tender sound?
To hearts familiar with the skies,
    The stars are nearer than the ground.

A BIRD'S-EYE VIEW.

Quoth the boy, " I'll climb that tree,
  And bring down a nest I know."
Quoth the girl, " I will not see
  Little birds defrauded so.
Cowardly their nests to take,
And their little hearts to break,
And their little eggs to steal.
  Leave them happy for my sake,—
Surely little birds can feel!"

Quoth the boy, " My senses whirl;
   Until now I never heard
Of the wisdom of a girl,
   Or the feelings of a bird !
Pretty Mrs. Solomon,
Tell me what you reckon on
When you prate in such a strain ;
   If I wring their necks anon,
Certainly they *might* feel—pain!"

Quoth the girl, " I watch them talk,
   Making love and making fun,
In the pretty ash-tree walk,
   When my daily task is done.
In their little eyes I find
They are very fond and kind.
Every change of song or voice,

Plainly proveth to my mind,
They can suffer and rejoice."

And the little Robin-bird
   (Nice brown back and crimson breast)
All the conversation heard,
   Sitting trembling in his nest.
What a world," he cried, " of bliss,
Full of birds and girls, were this !
Blithe we'd answer to their call ;
   But a great mistake it is
Boys were ever made at all."

A DAY'S FISHING.

Down by the pier, when the sweet morn
    is blowing,
  Slips from her moorings the fisher's
    light bark,
Sends up her ringing sails while she is
    going,
  Spread on the skies like the wings of
    the Dark!

F

Treads very timidly, pauses, grows
    bolder,
    Parts the soft wave like a tress from
    her brows,
Turns, like a girl looking over her
    shoulder,
    Poised in the dance, as she passes and
    bows.

There, while his slow net is swinging
    and sinking,
    There sits the fisher, a busy man
    he;
There, too, his little son, looking and
    thinking,
    Dumb with the joy of his first day at
    sea.

He thinks there are flowers for his small
    hands to gather,
  Down far below, if he only could
    dive;
He thinks that the fishes are friends of
    his father,
  And flock to his net like the bees to
    a hive.

He thinks that their yawl is a fortress
    unfailing,
  And, should he fall out, why, for cer-
    tain he floats;
He thinks that the sea was created for
    sailing,
  And wonders why spaces are left
    without boats.

He thinks that God made the salt water
    so bitter
  Lest folk should grow thirsty and
    drain the big cup;
He thinks that the foam makes a terrible
    litter,
  And wonders the mermaids don't
    sweep it all up.

He thinks if his father were half a life
    younger,
  What fun they might have with the
    coils of that rope;
He thinks—just a little—of cold and of
    hunger,
  And home—just a little—comes into
    his hope.

He fancies the hours are beginning to
 linger,
  Then looks with a pang at the down-
  dropping light,
And touches the sail with his poor little
 finger,
  And thinks it won't do for a blanket
  to-night.

The waves all around him grow blacker
 and vaster,
  He fears in his soul they are losing
  their way;
The darkness is hunting him faster and
 faster,
  And *the man there* sits watching him,
  gloomy and grey.

Oh ! is it his father? Oh ! where are they
     steering ?
  The changes of twilight are fatal and
     grim ;
And what is the place they are rapidly
     nearing,
  And whence are these phantoms so
     furious and dim ?

He is toss'd to the shore,—in a moment
     they grasp him,—
  One moment of horror, that melts
     into bliss !
It is but the arms of his mother that
     clasp him,
  His sobs and his laughter are lost in
     her kiss.

Page 70

Softly she welcomes her wandering trea-
    sure,
  " And *were* you afraid? Have I got
    you again?
Forget all the pain that came after your
    pleasure,
  In the rest and the peace that come
    after your pain."

DEAF AND DUMB.

HE lies on the grass, looking up to the
    sky;
Blue butterflies pass like a breath or a
    sigh,
The shy little hare runs confidingly
    near,
And wise rabbits stare with inquiry not
    fear,

Gay squirrels have found him and made
    him their choice ;
All creatures flock round him, and seem
    to rejoice.

Wild ladybirds leap on his cheeks fresh
    and fair,
Young partridges creep, nestling under
    his hair,
Brown honey-bees drop something sweet
    on his lips,
Rash grasshoppers hop on his round
    finger-tips,
Birds hover above him with musical
    call ;
All things seem to love him, and he
    loves them all.

Is nothing afraid of the boy lying
    there?
Would all nature aid if he wanted its
    care?
Things timid and wild with soft eager-
    ness come.
Ah, poor little child!—he is deaf—he
    is dumb.
But what can have brought them? but
    how can they know?
What instinct has taught them to cher-
    ish him so?

Since first he could walk they have
    served him like this.
His lips could not talk, but they found
    they could kiss.

They made him a court, and they
    crown'd him a king;
Ah, who could have thought of so love-
    ly a thing?
They found him so pretty, they gave
    him their hearts,
And some divine pity has taught them
    their parts!

A BIRTHDAY PETITION TO
A BUTTERFLY.

EVERYBODY must kiss me!
  It is my birthday to-day;
Soon, very soon they will miss me,
  So I can't linger to play.
But I ran out for a minute,
  One little kiss to implore;
Butterfly, once you begin it,
  Maybe you'll ask *me* for more!

Page 76

With all the blossoms coquetting,
　　Just at the close of the day,
You disappear at sunsetting;
　　Where do you flutter away?
Somebody made the suggestion,
　　Up to the stars you had flown;
Butterfly, answer my question,
　　Have you a star of your own?

Oft have I search'd for your dwelling,
　　And when I've seen you at rest,
Fancied the rose you were smelling
　　Might be a butterfly's nest.
Pray do you sleep with your dress on?
　　Have you your bed in a star?
(Do you believe, with my lesson,
　　That they are ever so far?)

Long for my birthday I've waited,
　　All of a sudden it's here!
Then I am petted and fêted
　　One royal day in the year!
Lessons no more are imparted,
　　Pleasure each moment must bring;
No one is half so hard-hearted
　　As to refuse me a thing!

Butterfly, *you* owe me duty,
　　Long have I waited for this;
Come in, you glittering beauty,
　　Give me a sweet little kiss.
Nobody dares to distress me;
　　You must be amiable too—
Butterfly, come and caress me,
　　I'll never tell if you do!

HEROES.

CHILDREN, when you sat wishing,
    Down last night on the sands,
Beckoning moments of glory,
    With little helpless hands,
I heard you saying and sighing,
    As the wind went over the seas,
"There never will come knights-errant
    To common days like these!"

I heard you sighing and saying,
  " The beautiful time is gone
When heroes hunted for monsters,
  and conquer'd them one by one;
And now there is nothing noble,
  And we all lie safe at night,
But we would not mind a monster
  If we could have a knight !"

Then taking breath for a moment,
  You all stood up and said,
" Remember Garibaldi !
  Not all the knights are dead :
A chief for men to follow,
  Who never lingers nor halts ;
A king for women and children,
  Because he has no faults.

" But he is nothing to England !
    There is the thought that smarts ;
We want an English hero,
    To trouble all our hearts."
Ah, children ! who could tell you
    That hearts grow sick and cold,
Without the healing trouble
    That touch'd the waters of old !

Shake not your heads at England,
    Her soil is still of worth ;
It cannot lose the habit
    Of bringing heroes forth.
I met one yesterday evening,
    And when you hear his tale,
You'll not be sighing and saying
    That times are feeble and pale.

G

The wind was soft and heavy,
  Where African palm-trees tower,
Hardly stirring the river,
  Hardly shaking a flower ;
The night was grave and splendid,
  A dead queen lying in state,
With all her jewels upon her,
  And trumpets at her gate.

The wild notes waved and linger'd,
  And fainted along the air,
Sometimes like defiance,
  And sometimes like despair ;
When down the moonlit mountain,
  And beside the river-calms,
The line of a dismal procession,
  Unwound between the palms.

A train of driven captives,
　　Weary, weak, amazed,—
Eighty hopeless faces,
　　Never once upraised ;
Bleeding from the journey,
　　Longing for the grave :
Men and women and children,
　　Every one a slave.

Lash'd and crying and crouching,
　　They pass'd, suspecting not
There were three or four English
　　Whose hearts grew very hot,—
Men who had come from a distance,
　　Whose lives were in their hands,
To tell the love of Jesus
　　About the heathen lands,

Studious men and gentle,
  But not in the least afraid;
With fire enough amongst them
  To furnish a crusade.
And when they saw the slave-troop
  Come hurrying down the hill,
Each man look'd at the other,
  Unable to be still.

They did not care for treaties,
  And death they did not fear;
One great wrong would have roused
    them,—
  There were eighty here.
They were not doing man's work,
  They were doing the Lord's,
So they went and stopp'd the savages
  With these amazing words:—

Page 84

" We are three or four English,
　　And we CANNOT LET THIS BE,—
Get away to your mountains,
　　And set the people free!"
You should have seen the black men,
　　How grey their faces turn;
They think the name of England
　　Is something that will burn.

They break, they fly like water
　　In a rushing, mighty wind;
The slaves stretch out uncertain hands,
　　By long despair made blind,
Till in a wonderful moment
　　The gasp of freedom came,
Like the leap of a tropical sunrise,
　　That sets the world aflame.

A blast of weeping and shouting
  Cleansed all the guilty place;
And God was able to undraw
  The curtain from His Face.
A hundred years of preaching
  Could not proclaim the creed
Of Love and Power and Pity
  So well as that one deed.

A glorious gift is Prudence;
  And they are useful friends
Who never make beginnings
  Till they can see the ends;
But give us now and then a man,
  That we may make him king,
Just to scorn the consequence,
  And just to DO THE THING.

A FANCY.

SHE placed the pitcher on her head,
   With idle steps the way she took
Across the pleasant field that led
   Down to the happy brook.
The summer breeze was all her own,
   The new-mown hay was sweet for her,
The birds sang in the very tone
   They knew she would prefer.

Her thoughts are hardly thoughts at all,
  So dream-like through her brain they
Her little feet do rise and fall   [flit ;
  Without her knowi g it.
The spirit of the twilight eve,
  Vague, beautiful, and purposeless,
Forbiddeth aught to vex or grieve,
  And doth in silence bless.

She standeth by the brook, she sees
  How smooth its roughest ripples are ;
The leafy murmur of the trees
  Makes melody afar.
A cloud can never mar the skies ;
  The sun can never rise again ;
A thought of change would bring sur-
    prise,
  And be a thought of pain.

Ah, child! the years that form thy past
  Are redolent with joys of spring!
The coming years are coming fast;
  Alas! what will they bring?
One hour is thine divinely dear,
  Enjoy it for its priceless good;
'Tis when thy childhood is as near
  As is thy womanhood!

THE SEASONS.

SPRING AND SUMMER.

SPRING is growing up,
   Is not it a pity?
She was such a little thing,
   And so very pretty!
Summer is extremely grand,
   We must pay her duty.
(But it is to little Spring
   That she owes her beauty!)

All the buds are blown,
   Trees are dark and shady,
(It was Spring who dress'd them, though,
   Such a little lady!)
And the birds sing loud and sweet
   Their enchanting hist'ries.
(It was Spring who taught them, though,
   Such a singing mistress!)

From the glowing sky
   Summer shines above us;
Spring was such a little dear,
   But will Summer love us?
She is very beautiful,
   With her grown-up blisses,
Summer we must bow before;
   Spring we coax'd with kisses!

Spring is growing up,
  Leaving us so lonely,
In the place of little Spring
  We have Summer only !
Summer, with her lofty airs,
  And her stately paces,
In the place of little Spring,
  With her childish graces !

AUTUMN.

Why do the pretty flow'rs die?
  Butterflies ought to protect them !
What is the use of the sun and the sky
  Tempting them out to neglect them ?
Honey-bee, Honey-bee, why don't you
    come ?
  Look at the sorrowful border !

It is so seifish to dawdle and hum,
  When you might keep things in
    order.

Blame not the poor busy bees,
  Merchants for traffic and buying;
Sweet idle butterflies do as they please,
  They might keep blossoms from dying.
All pretty secrets are hid in the sky,
  Flying up there they must know
    them,
How can the flow'rs find the way *not* to
    die,
  Unless the butterflies show them?

Shame on the butterflies! How
  Can they look buds in their faces?

Poor little lives that must drop from the
    bough,
    Leaving no definite traces.
Hush! the bees murmur, the butterflies
    speak,
    Crying aloud we must hear them;
I'll be so glad if the hearing they seek
    From all suspicion can clear them.

Well—they declare it is *we*
    Who are so blind and conceited,
Not understanding the work that we see
    Till it is done and completed.
Over mock funerals making our moan,
    For pretty favourites sighing,
Who, when Spring comes, will compel
    us to own
    They had not a notion of dying!

WINTER.

Wonderful white Winter!
   I must clap my hands at you;
You are old and I am cold,
   And there is nothing else to do.
You and I are glad, are glad
   When the snow comes creeping down,
And icedrops fair leap out of the air
   To hang on the branches brown!

Wonderful white Winter!
   It is when you first begin
With berries fine the churches shine—
   That is how we bring you in.
Don't you love the ding-dong bells?
   Don't you love the hearty cheer?
The merry blaze, the good old plays,
   When you fetch the little new year?

Wonderful white Winter!
  Wave your lovely snow-white hand;
Signal make till river and lake
  Form the ice that is so grand!
Oh, the ice is dear, is dear;
  Faithless friend, changed by a breath,
Smooth and sweet to gliding feet,
  Gliding over grim death!

Wonderful white Winter!
  I will make a league with you;
You must know of want and woe,
  Tell me what I ought to do!
I must feed you little birds?
  Shelter to the homeless lend?
Comfort and aid the poor and afraid?
  That I will, my brave old friend!

Page 96

THE LADY AND THE ROOKS.

TRUST the grand and gentle trees,
　　Never will their welcome fade;
All that lives may lie at ease
　　In the haven of their shade;
Treasuries of tranquil air
　　Keep they for the burning days;
And their boughs ascend like prayer,
　　And their leaves break forth like
　　　praise.

H

Patient are they, for they wait
   On the humours of the year;
Noble, for they keep their state
   When the winter leaves them sere;
Brave to suffer heat and cold,
   And the tempest's war-alarms;
Very tender, for they hold
   All bird-babies in their arms.

Where the winter silence hears
   No voice louder than a brook's,
There was built for many years
   A great city of the rooks;
There they brush the tall elm-crests
   With their sable waft of wing;
You may count a hundred nests,
   Bare among the buds of spring.

Couch'd in crimson window-curve,
   Looks a lady to the sky,
Sees each builder swoop and swerve,
   Like a great black butterfly;
Hum of their familiar talk,
   Brings a greeting to her ear,
WE are in the elm-tree walk!
   Spring is sure, and summer near!

But a louder note invades,
   Whence and how? who dares to tell?
They are building in the shades,
   By her own pet oriel!
In her cedar, which so long
   With a separate glory stood,
Like a Sunday-tree among
   Work-day brethren of the wood.

In her cedar—nothing less !
   Heavens, what free-and-easy birds !
Now she utters her distress,
   Loudly, with despotic words :—
" This is quite against the laws,
   You must drive them out of reach ;
We shall have superfluous caws
   Mixing with our parts of speech."

So she spake, and it was done ;
   Strew the ruins at her feet !
Little homestead, scarce begun,
   You shall never be complete.
See how silent and dismay'd
   Hang the guilty pair aloof ;
Tenants they, with rent unpaid,
   Watching their dismantled roof.

And the fair spring-day was lost
  In a soft prophetic night,
Covering all the coming host
  Of King Summer's bloom and light ;
And the household lay at rest,
  Dreaming not of labour vain ;
And the rooks to that poor nest
  Came and set to work again.

Angry eyes awoke and saw,
  Ruthless hands the work undo ;
Many a faint remonstrant caw
  Dies unheeded in the dew.
Five times was the nest begun ;
  Five times, with the dawn of day,
Were the cunning links undone,
  And the framers chased away.

But one night, through all the trees,
    Went a whirr of wings afloat,
And a tumult and a breeze,
    Big with caws from many a throat;
Sleep is hunted from the house;
    Through the dark the master looks,
Saying to his weary spouse,
    " There's a strike among the rooks."

To that houseless pair forlorn
    All the nation came in aid :
" This," they cried, " cannot be borne;
    " In a night it shall be made !"
And it was !   They pile, they weave,
    Flit, fuss, chatter through the shade;
The first twig was set at eve,
    And by dawn the eggs were laid.

When the lady came to see,
　　Much she marvell'd, as she might,
Such a goodly work to be
　　Finish'd in a single night.
All the air was black with wings,
　　For the nation hover'd near,
Pleading for their precious things,
　　Half in anger, half in fear.

THE ROOKS' PETITION.

"Bear with us! Your garden shows
　　Many a snug and comely nest;
But the very leaf we chose
　　Is for us the only best;
And you would not wish a change
　　In the music of our words,

If you knew how harsh and strange
　　Seems *your* talk to all the birds !

" We are happy where we please,
　　Not where you would have us dwell ;
We've our choice among the trees,—
　　You, your own pet oriel.
If you hunt us while we sue,
　　You are strong, and we despair ;
But one thing you cannot do,
　　Make us feel at home elsewhere.

" Rulers to their cost have found,
　　Hearts of men are much like ours ;
Laws that grow not from the ground
　　Often die like gather'd flowers.
Rule and measure as they may,
　　They will find at last perhaps,

God makes pictures every day
    Which are better things than maps.

" But we wander from our text,—
    We are most discursive birds,
And your eyes, although perplex'd,
    Seem to soften at our words.
Yes, they soften, they forgive
    Even a constancy misplaced ;
Granting humblest things that live
    Whim and fancy, wish and taste !"

THE SICK CHILD.

BIRD, are you singing to me,
    Perch'd on my own window-sill?
Can you, in your little brain,
Knowledge have and thought retain,
That I am lying here in pain,
    Weary, weak, and ill?
Is that pretty music mine?
    Sweeter I have never heard;

Page 106

As each pleasant little note
Leaps from your exultant throat,
Like the sun they seem to shine,
    Oh, you friendly bird!

Bird, are you singing to me?
    Singing of wood and of dell?
Of the flowers I used to take,
Of the nut-trees I would shake,
Of the fishing on the lake,
    Have you come to tell?
Singing, singing joyfully,
    Joyfully my heart is stirr'd.
None so blithe and brave as I,
Standing 'neath my own blue sky,
Such the dream you bring to me,
    You delightful bird.

Bird, are you singing to me?
　　Ah, but the winter is near!
Then your foot will find no rest,
And the snow will be your nest;
You will seek, with beak distrest,
　　Food that is not here.
Faithful to our friendship I—
　　You may take me at my word—
Bread and milk shall greet you still
At this pleasant window-sill,
That you never yet flew by,
　　Darling little bird.

A DREAM OF THE WAR.

FORGET-ME-NOTS grow by the stream,
   Their blue eyes look up to the skies;
I think I have seen in a dream
   As blue and as beautiful eyes!
The brooklet runs quivering on,
   Its little waves glitter and gleam;
In my dreams I have seen such a one,
   But it was not a brook in my dream.
On the bank of the brooklet I lay,
   And gather'd the little blue stars,

And I thought of the men far away,
  Who were fighting for me in the wars.
Who were fighting for me and for you,
  'Mid dangers that well might appall :
All hearts should to soldiers be true,
  For they offer their lives for us all !

He came, with his poor wooden leg,
  His arm was tied up in a sling,
He never attempted to beg,
  And look'd just as proud as a king !
He was young, and my heart bled for
    that ;
  He was poor—tatter'd coat and torn
    boot ;
Two fingers went up to his hat,
  And he gave me a soldier's salute.

" Ah, soldier!" I cried, " is it so?
   Have you come from the wars far
     away,
Where you fought for me bravely, I
     know,
   And your life was go gallant and gay !
Poor, wounded, disabled, alone,
   But how inexpressibly dear !
Take all I can give, 'tis your own,—
   Food, shelter, and money are here."

He look'd at me sadly, and smiled ;
   He said, " To my home I must creep ;
I have got such a dear little child,
   Whom I only have seen in my sleep!
My wife thinks the moments are long'
   She watches and waits in our cot ;

She loved me when stately and strong,
    She will love me more now,—will
        she not?

" I do not believe I shall die,
    Though carried as dead from the
        fight."
I eagerly cried, " Nor do I !
    I pray'd for you morning and night !
In every church through the land
    Have prayers for your welfare been
        said."
He answer'd, " I don't understand—
    Who cared if I lived or were dead ?"

Ah, soldier ! you fought for us all ;
    Each woman and child was your care ;

And England replied to the call,
  And thought of each man in her
    prayer.
In churches and homes where we knelt,
  And prayers with our very hearts
For *every* soldier we felt,   [made,
  For *every* soldier we pray'd !

To the soul of the loyal and brave,
  The love of his country is sweet.
The brooklet flow'd on like a wave;
  The Forget-me-nots fell at his feet.
My heart seem'd to quiver and beat,
  The brooklet to glitter and gleam;
The Forget-me-nots fell at the feet
  Of the soldier I saw in my dream !

CHILDREN ON THE SHORE.

WE are building little homes on the
    sands,
  We are making little rooms very gay,
We are busy with our hearts and our
    hands,
  We are sorry that the time flits away.
Oh, why are the minutes in such haste?
  Oh, why won't they leave us to our
    play?

Our lessons and our meals are such
    waste!
  We can dine very well another day.

We do not mind the tide coming in,—
  We can dig it a cunning little bed,
Or leave our pretty house and begin
  Another pretty house in its stead;
We do not mind the sun in our eyes,
  When it makes such a dazzle of the
    world,
That we cannot tell the sea from the
  skies,
  Nor look where the flying drops are
    hurl'd.

The shells that we gather are so fair,
  The birds and the clouds are so kind,

And the wind is so merry with our hair,—
　　It is only the *People* that we mind!
Papa, if you come so very near,
　　We can't build the library to-day;
We think you are tired of being here,
　　And, perhaps, you would like to go
　　　　away.

There are just one or two we won't re-
　　fuse,
　　If they come by, to help us now and
　　　　then;
But we want only friends to be of use,
　　And not all those idle grown-up men;
Perhaps, if we hurry very much,
　　And don't lose an instant of the day,
There'll be time for the last lovely touch
　　Before the sea sweeps it all away.

Oh, children—thus working with the
    heart!
  There's nothing so terrible as rest;
Plan only how all may take a part:
  It's easy for each to do his best.
The sea, sweeping up at set of sun,
  Can never make your toil be in vain;
It covers the things that you have done,
  But the joy of the doing shall remain!

THE SNOW-DOG.

SHE has not a morsel to eat !
  Just fancy a child in that state,
Creeping along all alone in the street,
  A sweet little creature of eight.
The mansion is splendidly lit,
  The supper is shining through flowers,
But the poor little child has not tasted
    .a bit
  For twenty-four terrible hours.

She lays herself down at the door,
　　She curls herself up in a heap,
She thinks that this world is too hard
　　　for the poor,
　　And hopes she may die in her sleep !
So soft, uncomplaining, and small,
　　So delicate, slender, and mild,
She lies at the door of the beautiful hall
　　A poor, little, desolate child !

Who opens the door bright and gay ?
　　Who shouts like a hero at least ?
Why, who could it be but the lord of the
　　　day—
　　The birthday-boy, king of the feast !
Rich velvet envelopes his form ;
　　His face is a smiling full-moon ;

His golden curls flicker about in the
    storm ;
  His laughter rings out like a tune !

A snow-covered heap in the street.
  He sees it, nor quite understands ;
He pushes it on with his wee, dainty
    feet,
  And clasps his dear, mischievous hands.
He cries, " Oh, what happiness !   Oh,
  This birthday-gift's nicest by far.
Hurrah ! here's a beautiful dog in the
    snow—
  A beautiful snow-dog, hurrah !"

He drags her along in his glee,   [light,
  Through chambers of splendour and

Still crying, " My snow-dog—and are
    you for me,
  With your girl's face so pretty and
    white ?"
Ah, child! prize this birthday-gift, 'tis
  More precious than gold can pro-
    cure.
The good God himself, dear, has given
    you this,—
  The good God that takes care of the
    poor.

How pleasantly warm is the fire!
  How soft is the rug where she lies!
Oh, what is there left for her heart to
    desire,
  As she opens her tremulous eyes?

They feed her with delicate things,
　　She laughs that her troubles are past;
She thinks they are angels, she looks
　　for their wings,
　　And hopes it is heaven at last!

FEEDING THE FAIRIES.

Fairies, fairies, come and be fed,
 Come and be fed like hens and cocks;
Hither and thither with delicate tread,
 Flutter around me in fairy flocks.
Come, little fairies, from far and near;
 Come, little fairies, I know you can fly;
Who can be dear if *you* are not dear?
 And who is so fond of a fairy as *I?*

Fairies, fairies, come if you please,
  Nod your heads and ruffle your wings,
Marching in order or standing at ease,
  Frolicsome fairies are dear little things!
Golden the grain and silver the rice,
  Pleasant the crumbs from Mama's
    own bread,
Currants pick'd out of the pudding are
    nice—
  Fairies, fairies, come and be fed!

Hushaby, oh! hushaby, oh!
  Hide by the door—keep very still—
I must be gentle, I must speak low,
  Or frighten the fairies I certainly will.
Fairies are easily frighten'd, I know;
  They are so small, we must pity their
    fears.

Hushaby, oh! hushaby, oh!
  Coax them and humour them—poor
    little dears!

Fairies, fairies, why don't you come?
  Fairies, fairies, wherefore delay?
In a few minutes I must run home—
  Cross little creatures! you know I
    can't stay!
See how I scatter your beautiful food—
  Good little fairies would come when
    I call;
Fairies, fairies, *won't* you be good?
  What is the use of my speaking at all?

IN THE FIELDS.

AIRY budding ash-tree,
   You have made a throne,
And the sweetest thrush in all the world
   Is sitting there alone;
Drawn in tints of tender brown
   Against a keen blue sky,
He sings up and he sings down,
   Who can pass him by?

Through the thin leaves thrilling
  Goes each glittering note,
Hearts of all happy trees are drawn
  Into this one bird-throat;
And all the growing blooms of morn
  (This music is so strong)
Are reach'd and blended and upborne
  And utter'd into song.

Now he asks a question !
  The answer who can guess—
While sparrows chirp their pettish "No,"
  And daws keep murmuring " Yes " ?
" Oh, will the months be kind and clear,
  Unvex'd by needless rain ;
And will the Summer last this year
  Till Spring comes back again ?"

Now he states a dogma !
  His view of day and night;
Proclaiming volubly and loud
  No other bird is right.   [checks
But halfway through his creed he
  At some sweet chance of sound,
And, catching that, no longer recks
  If heaven or earth go round.

Now he labours gravely,
  Each moment pays itself,
No singer ever work'd so hard
  For art or fame or pelf;
And now he knows the pretty phrase
  And scatters it like rain,
With quick " Da Capos " of self-praise,
  Till the tree rings again.

He pleads, he laughs, he argues,
   He shouts to sky and earth;
The wild notes trip each other up
   In ecstasies of mirth;
He drinks the azure of the air,
   He tosses song about,
Like a girl's tangle of gold-hair,
   Spray-wet and shaken out.

O world! when spring is shining
   And dark winds stand aside,
Let men think of you as they may,
   The birds are satisfied;
Their dauntless hymns of hope arise
   With such a wealth of will;
Though every year the summer dies,
   They trust her promise still.

K

Airy budding ash-tree,
  Try to show your power,
Make a leaf for each gay note
  He makes in half an hour!
Wild flowers in the grass, be taught
  The music of your parts;
Make a bud for each bright thought
  He gives to passing hearts!

DISOBEDIENCE.

Says he, " I'll take my father's gun,
   Obedience is absurd;
And would not it be awful fun
   If I could shoot a bird !"
Says she, " A bird you cannot shoot."
   Says he, " But, if I can ?"
Says she, " You'll feel just like a brute."
   Says he, " No; like a man !"

" And when my father shoots," says he;
  " Who speaks a word of blame?
And very 'cute that bird must be
  That can elude his aim!
And am not I, my father's son,
  Heir to my father's skill?
Says you—You shall not touch his gun,
  Says I,—Bedad, I will!"

Says she, " Your honour you forget;
  What! do it on the sly?"
Says he, " That little sermonet
  Is *really* all my eye!
For if a fellow went to speak
  And promulgate such views,
You'd be the first to call it 'cheek,'
  And tremble in your shoes!"

" And with my faithful comrade Shag,
  (Dear dog, beloved of all!),
I rather think I'll fill a bag,
  That's the reverse of small;
The noble dog looks in my face
  With his true, honest eyes,
And wags his tail with placid grace,
  And barks his glad surprise."

Then with that merry laugh of his
  He waved the gun on high,
And sang, " Ye birds, that whirr and
  Ye little think it's I!   [whiz,
Ye birds that whiz and whirr for me,
  That whirr and whiz," he sang,
" I've got my father's gun, you see,
  And *won't* I make it bang!"

Oh! when the wrong we once begin,
  How can we grasp the right?
He thought it such a little sin,
  And such a large delight;
He thought it such a little sin,
  A merry 'lark' at most;
But when the wrong we once begin,
  How can we count the cost?

A movement indolent and rash,
  Half earnest, half in joke,
A sudden shock, a deadly crash,
  A cloud of lurid smoke—
The noble dog lies there in pain,
  His life-blood streaming fast.
Oh! life that cannot come again,
  Soon reckon'd with the past!

The noble dog looks up at him
   With his true honest eyes,
Poor eyes that now are waxing dim,
   Large limbs that may not rise;
The friendly ever-wagging tail
   Moves faintly to and fro;
In life or death Shag could not fail
   To greet his master so!

In mute despair his master stands,
   Wishing his work undone;
The gun has fallen from his hands,
   The wicked, tempting gun!
He kneels beside him on the floor,
   Striving to soothe his pain;
If tears and kisses could restore,
   Poor Shag would live again!

Too late, with vain remorse, he sees
   The fault that wrought the ill;
Had he obey'd his sire's decrees,
   Shag had been living still!
Poor Shag! who seems to understand
   The sorrow in his eyes,
And kindly licks his master's hand,
   Though by that hand he dies.

Oh, children! in these days of ours
   Fairies have vanishèd,
I think that they have lost their powers,—
   I fear they all are dead.
But when this boy was doing wrong
   (Which its own sorrow brings),
Fairies were very young and strong,
   And did amazing things!

So when he bound the bleeding side,
　　And kiss'd the fainting nose,
Just when poor Shaggie should have died
　　The fairies interpose!
But, children, *we* must recollect
　　Fairies no more appear;
If *we* do wrong, we must expect
　　That it will cost us dear!

And though Shag's wound was soon
　　　forgot,
　　The boy was still to blame;
And had poor Shaggie ne'er been shot,
　　The fault was still the same!
Whate'er may be the consequence,
　　Whether we lose or win,
The sin of disobedience
　　Is a most fearful sin.

LILIES.

A CHILD is lying fast asleep
   Down where the lilies grow,
And the lilies nod and peep,
   Quite pleased to have him so.
And the lilies softly say,
   "We must not sleep, you know,
Lest he wake and run away,
   Fast as little legs can go."

Page 138

Lilies are so innocent,
   Sorrow they never knew;
How can lily-flowers repent
   As thorny roses do?
And a little child asleep,
   Fresh as a drop of dew,
With emotion soft and deep
   Thrills a lily through and through!

If a tender smile he give,
   Or stretcheth out his hand,
(Bright the dreams that for him live,
   Kept safe in Heaven-land!)
Eager lilies forward press,
   Bending their blossoms grand;
Blossoms that have power to bless
   Only children understand.

They shake their pretty heads,
　　Rustling and whispering,
" Children ought to be in beds,
　　For birds have ceased to sing.
Every bird is in its bush,
　　Its head beneath its wing;
Will the birds be angry? hush!
　　Don't speak of such a thing!

" We will hide him if we can,
　　He shan't be seen or heard
We can face an angry man,
　　But *not* an angry bird!
We are getting frighten'd!　Oh,
　　Surely the branches stirr'd!
Shall we waken him? ah, no!
　　What might not be inferr'd?"

Two wide-open eyes of blue
    Look'd up at them and smiled:
" Why what could the birdies do,
    That are so soft and mild?
Foolish lilies, rouse your powers,
    Please do not talk so wild;
Don't you know that birds and flowers
    Love every little child?"

PUCK.

She is sleeping on the grass,
Where her daily footsteps pass;
All her errands left undone
At the bidding of the sun;
From the glory of whose ray
Shining eyes are hid away.
　　And, for aught that we can tell,
Little shining eyes were made,

Like the glowworm in the dell,
Only to illumine shade!

Pretty Puck, the farmyard's pride,
Grazeth calmly at her side;
Fat wee Puck, who harsher word
Than "Gee up" has never heard!
Nice white bread and apples good
May be call'd his daily food.
Pleasant pats instead of blows,
    Recompense him if he trips;
And on his expectant nose,
    Kisses from her rosy lips.

Happily the maiden sleeps
Nearer and nearer danger creeps;
Placidly the pony eats
Dewy moss and grassy sweets;

Loathsome thing of craft and fear
Creepeth nearer and more near,—-
Crafty, faithless, slimy, slim,
   Slipping on with noiseless stir;
Wilily it passeth him,
   Swiftly it approacheth her!

Its vile head is raised on high,
Cunning triumph in its eye;
Open jaws that long tb shed
All their poison on her head;
Happy hearts would bleed and break
At thy deed, detested snake.
But with gesture wild and proud,
   Oh, wise Puck! oh, trusty Puck!
Stamps his foot and neighs aloud,
   Ere the venom'd tongue can suck!

Lightly through the trembling grass
Doth the baffled creature pass,
Baffled in its vile intent,
Hungry spite its punishment!
Back to life and all its joys
Comes the maiden at the noise,
Blaming naughty Puck for this.
   Ah! she little, little knows,
Life itself, with all its bliss,
    Unto naughty Puck she owes!

So it is, we *cannot* know
All to that dumb world we owe.
What we do for them they see,
Blind and less enlighten'd, we!
We may punish or caress,
But the truth we cannot guess.

L

Silent hearts may every day,
  By the instinct of their love,
Scatter blessings on our way,
  Countless dangers may remove.

Will such acts in life unknown
Ever to our eyes be shown,
Till at last we see how far
They our benefactors are,
And that we must abdicate
Something of our fancied state?
And if this indeed could be
  (Somewhere else than in my dreams),
We should learn humility,
  Which so hard a lesson seems.

RAIN AFTER DROUGHT.

A WIND came out of the Moon's clear
  heart,
 Straight and soft in my face it blew;
It was not cold, but it made me start,
 And think of something new.
What is coming? A thunder-cloud
 To cover the wild, white sky
With a great procession purple and proud,
 And a whirlwind flashing by?

It is only the tender, musical rain
Coming to comfort earth again !

Hark, it is here !   There's joy, indeed,
    And work in the deeps below ;
Every drop finds out a seed,
    And tells it how to grow.
The fever of the grass is heal'd,
    The thirsty roots revive,
A whisper runs about the field,
    That daisies are alive ;
All make ready a glad surprise
For anxious Day's returning eyes.

Little he thought when he went to rest
    What Night was going to do !
He had been watching a world oppress'd,
    And now all things are new.

Now let him shine with all his might
  On river and plain and bough,
Eyes that wearily ached last night
  Will only glitter now.
Day, you never can last too long—
Day, you are welcome, for Earth is
    strong !

THE MERMAID.

THE moon is in the sky, and the stars
    are shining too,
The summer-night is calm, and the sea
    is very blue;
The sea is very blue, and the radiance
    of the moon
Is playing on the waves like a lovely
    floating tune!

Upon a sea-girt rock a lonely mermaid
    stands,
She murmurs to the sea, and she wrings
    her little hands;
She wrings her little hands, and she
    murmurs o'er and o'er,
" Alas for me! I *wish* that I lived upon
    the shore!

" The sea is very cold, it makes me
    shiver so,
And I do not like the fish that about
    me come and go;
I do not like the fish—they swim so
    very near,
And the large ones leap and tumble,
    and fill my heart with fear.

" How horrible the creatures that are
    round me everywhere !
Oh, why do mortals take them and keep
    them with such care ?
They do not heed the pretty grass that
    scenteth wood and dell,
But they pluck my sea anemones with
    their horrid fishy smell.

" Oh, dismal are the caverns beneath the
    foaming waves,
And dismal are the mermen who live
    within those caves !
And the slimy, slimy seaweeds that
    round them cling and grow,
And the dropping, dropping waters that
    make me shiver so !

" How beautiful the happy homes upon
　　the blessèd land !
How beautiful the blazing fires I hardly
　　understand !
But I should die contented if I once had
　　my desire,
To slumber on a downy couch beside a
　　blazing fire !

" And pretty on the downs are the tender
　　lambs and sheep,
And pretty are the little dogs that run
　　about and leap ;
But when the children come and play
　　upon the silver sand,
I cry—' Alas, for me !—I *wish* I lived
　　upon the land !'

"And then on summer evenings, Oh,
    what enchanting bliss,
To wander amid green, green woods on
    such a night as this!
With the blue heavens above your head
    that always tranquil lie,
Unlike the restless, leaping waves that
    form our troubled sky!"

Thus floated on the night breeze, on
    summer evenings long,
This lamentation, wild and strange, the
    lovely mermaid's song;
And still the burden was the same, re-
    peated o'er and o'er,
"Alas, for me!—I *wish* that I lived
    upon the shore!"

Page 31

THE FISHERMAN'S WIFE.

THE wind bloweth wildly; she stands
    on the shore;
  She shudders to hear it, and will ever-
    more.
The rush of the waves, as they rose and
    they fell,
  Evermore to her fancy will sound like
    a knell!

" When, mother, dear mother, will father
    return ?
   His supper is ready,—the sticks
    brightly burn ;
His chair is beside them, with dry shoes
    and coat,
   I'm longing to kiss him,—Oh, where
    is the boat ?

" Why does he not come with his fish
    on his arm ?
   He *must* want his supper,—he *can-*
    not be warm ;
I'll stroke his cold cheek, with his wet
    hair I'll play,
   I want so to kiss him,—Oh, why does
    he stay ?"

Unheeding the voice of that prattler,
    she stood
    To watch the wild war of the tempest
      and flood;
One little black speck in the distance
    doth float,
    'Tis her world—'tis her life—'tis her
      fisherman's boat!

Her poor heart beats madly 'twixt hope
    and despair,
    She watches his boat with a wild,
      glassy stare;
Ah! 'tis hid beneath torrents of silvery
    spray,
    Ah! 'tis buried mid chasms that yawn
      for their prey.

Over mountains of horrible waves it is
    tost,
  It is far—it is near—it is safe—*it is
  lost !*
The proud waves of ocean unheeding
    rush on,
  But, alas ! for the little black speck—
  it is gone !

Oh ! weep for the fisherman's boat, but
    weep more
  For the desolate woman who stands
  on the shore !
She flies to her home with a shrill cry of
    pain,
  To that home where her loved one
  returns not again.

All night she sits speechless, her child
    weeping near,
      But no sob shakes her bosom,—her
        eye feels no tear;
In heartbroken, motionless, stupid de-
    spair,
      She sits gazing on,—at his coat and
        his chair.

Hark! a click of the latch,—a hand
    opens the door,
      'Tis a step—her heart leaps—'tis *his*
        step on the floor;
He stands there before her all dripping
    and wet,
      But his smile and his kiss have warm
        life in them yet.

He is here, he is safe, though his boat
    is a wreck;
  He sinks in his chair—while her arms
    clasp his neck,
And a sweet little voice in his ear
    whispers this,
  "Do kiss me, dear father—I long for
    a kiss!"

MORNING.

How pleasant is the morning!
   How innocent and bright!
How pretty and surprising
To see the sun uprising,
   A ball of golden light!
While sleepy twilight melts away,
And the delicious summer day
   Succeeds the silent night!

How pleasant is the morning,
　　When birds with merry cry
Leap from their nests delighted,
Earth and its dwellers slighted,
　　Fling music at the sky!
Oh let me, birds, with you rejoice,
For, though less musical my voice,
　　A singing heart have I.

How pleasant is the morning!
　　The flowers begin to shine;
No longer idly dozing,
Their happy eyes unclosing,
　　Look laughing into mine.
I watch them open one by one,
Bidding good-morning to the sun
　　By many a pretty sign.

How pleasant is the morning!
   Dark night, I love thee not;
To lie in dreamless slumber
Through hours I cannot number
   Is childhood's hapless lot.
Lovely the moon and stars may be;
Their loveliness is not for me,
   In sleep they are forgot.

How pleasant is the morning!
   Bright earth and dewy sky
Delicious tears are weeping,
And rivulets are leaping,
   And breezes flutter by; [grass,
And birds and flowers and trees and
And changeful shadows as they pass,
   Enchant the eager eye.

How pleasant is the morning!
How bountiful is He
Who made delight a duty
And filled the earth with beauty,
And gave us eyes to see!
Rejoice, O happy world, rejoice,
And raise to Him thy merry voice,
Childhood serene and free.

EVENING.

It is the hour of evening
    When nature is at rest:
Each weary bird is sleeping
    Within its pleasant nest;
The bee hath ceased its humming,
    The fish no longer springs,
Even the happy butterfly
    Closeth its shining wings.

The pretty flowers are lying
   Half hidden in the grass;
They cannot hear our footsteps
   Or our voices as we pass.
For all their darling blossoms
   Are shut in slumber deep,
Just like the eyes of children
   When they are fast asleep!

The little stars are twinkling,
   See how they shine and shake;
The little stars are sleepy,
   They cannot keep awake.
The moon has hidden from us,
   She is so very proud;
But I know that she is sleeping
   Behind yon silver cloud.

It is the hour of evening,
    As all creation feels ;
The world is very beautiful
    While slumber o'er it steals.
No sound profanes the silence
    Of its unbroken peace,
But the flowing of the water
    That can never, never cease.

The flowing of the water
    Is a very sleepy sound ;
The lullaby of nature,
    With silence all around ;
The music of the night-time,
    It stealeth to repose.
The never resting water,
    How sleepily it flows !

BIRDS.

MANY voices in the woodlands
  Strike on the delighted ear,—
Voices from the trees above us
  Singing to the opening year;
Notes that seem to come from heaven
  Making earth and sky so near.

Little birds, serene and happy,
  Surely in your upward flight

Ye are touch'd with heaven's glory,
  Ye are bathed in heaven's light;
And its colours and its shadows
  Make you creatures of delight.

Little robin! little robin!
  Is the glow upon your breast
Only the reflected splendour
  Of the sunset in the west?
Hath the sunset tinged your bosom,
  Little bird that I love best?

Tell me, golden-coloured finches,
  Whose resplendent plumage vies
With the glory of the morning
  Just before the sunbeams rise,—
Is, indeed, your radiant colour
  Stolen from the Eastern skies?

Humming-bird and stately parrot,
  On your crests and on your wings
Rainbow hues are ever changing,
  Rainbow beauty ever clings ;
Have you visited the rainbow,
  Pretty, sparkling, painted things ?

But the little humble creatures
  (Very sweet their voices too !)
Who are wrapp'd in russet mantles,
  Like the clouds of sombre hue,—
Do you think *beneath* that shadow
  Is a garb of heaven's own blue ?

Do you think, to angels' glances
  They are clad like shining flowers,
And their hues are only gloomy
  Unto eyes as dull as ours ?

Oh, that we had humbler spirits,
  Purer hearts, and keener powers !

Little voices in the woodlands,
  Little creatures in the air,
Sweet it is at morn and evening,
  Music floating everywhere ;
Dear to me your little voices
  Kindling hope and soothing care.

THE LITTLE MAIDEN.

THERE was a little maiden,
  She was not six years old;
Blue were her eyes as summer skies,
  Her hair like burnish'd gold;
She took her wicker basket,
  With rosy ribbons twined,
And little Jane ran down the lane
  Wild strawberries to find.

There was a wicked gipsy,
   She met her in the glade;
She said, " Come here, my pretty dear,
   Oh, never be afraid!
I'll give you sugar-candy
   And cakes and comfits sweet;
Oh, come with me, and you shall see
   A most delightful treat."

Alas! that little maiden
   Believed each pleasant word,
She did not know of crime or woe,
   Of falsehood had not heard;
Her peaceful life was stranger
   To the very name of sin,
For love and truth did guard her youth,
   Her happy home within.

She look'd up at the gipsy
    With such a merry smile,
Her pretty eyes with glad surprise
    Are shining all the while;
Her tiny rosy fingers
    In that brown hand she laid;
They run so fast—they stop at last,
    Alas! poor little maid!

The wicked gipsy led her
    Into a dismal wood;
She took away her garments gay,
    Her scarlet cloak and hood;
But when in rags and tatters
    Her tender form was drest,
The little maid was not afraid,
    She thought it was a jest.

And now the sun is setting
  'Mid clouds of rosy light,
Soft shadows pass o'er moss and grass,
  Where dewdrops glitter bright;
She kneels before the gipsy
  And bends her pretty head,   [face,
With childish grace and sweet grave
  " I'll say my prayers," she said.

Her small hands claspt together,
  She whisper'd soft and mild,
" Pray God bless both my parents,
  And make me a good child.
And bless this dear old woman,
  For very kind is she;
I'll take her home, if she will come,
  Pray God bless her and me."

Ah, when the gipsy saw her,
   And heard her childish prayer,
Big tears arise into her eyes,
   Unwonted dwellers there.
She felt that she was sorry,
   And with the sorrow came
Repentance true—as it must do—
   And with repentance, shame.

The little maiden kiss'd her,
   And then fell fast asleep;
Like twilight rose, her eyelids close,
   Open they could not keep.
The gipsy raised her gently;
   With weariness and pain,
She set her face back to retrace
   Her wicked steps again.

To that dear home she bore her,
  Where mourners watch'd all night,
And still she slept while others wept
  With rapture and delight.
In her deserted nursery,
  Upon her own white bed,
They softly laid that little maid,
  And prayers above her said.

Ah, children! little children!
  Your innocence hath power:
The gipsy left the paths of theft
  From that eventful hour.
Repentant for past errors,
  She toil'd with honest care;
Ah, well she might bless day and night
  The little maiden's prayer!

RANGER.

A LITTLE boat in a cave,
  And a child there fast asleep;
Floating out on a wave,
  Out to the perilous deep—
Out to the living waters,
  That brightly dance and gleam,
And dash their foam about him,
  To wake him from his dream.

He rubs his pretty eyes,
　　He shakes his curly head,
And says, with great surprise,
　　" Why, I'm not asleep in bed!"
The boat is rising and sinking
　　Over the sailors' graves,
And he laughs out, " Isn't it nice,
　　Playing see-saw with the waves?"

Alas! he little thinks
　　Of the grief on the far-off sands,
Where his mother trembles and shrinks,
　　And his sister wrings her hands,
Watching in speechless terror,
　　The boat and the flaxen head.
Is there no hope of succour?
　　Must they see him drown'd and dead?

They see him living now,
    Living and jumping about;
He stands on the giddy prow,
    With a merry laugh and shout.
Oh, spare him! spare him! spare him!
    Spare him, thou cruel deep!
The child is swept from the prow,
    And the wild waves dance and leap.

They run to the edge of the shore,
    They stretch their arms to him;
Knee-deep they wade, and more,
    But, alas! they cannot swim.
Their pretty, pretty darling,
    His little hat floats by;
They see his frighten'd face;
    They hear his drowning cry.

Page 181

Something warm and strong
    Dashes before them then,
Hairy and curly and long,
    And brave as a dozen men;
Bounding—panting—gasping,
    Rushing straight as a dart;
· Ready to die in the cause,
    A dog with a loyal heart.

He fights with the fighting sea,
    He grandly wins his prize;
Mother! he brings it thee
    With triumph in his eyes.
He brings it thee, oh, mother!
    His burden, pretty and pale;
He lays it down at thy feet,
    And wags his honest old tail.

O dog! so faithful and bold;
   O dog! so tender and true;
You shall wear a collar of gold,
   And a crown, if you like it, too.
You shall lie on the softest satin;
   You shall feed from a diamond dish;
You shall eat plumcake and cream,
   And do whatever you wish.

Will you drive in a coach and four?
   Will you ride the master's hack?
Shall the footman open the door,
   And out of your presence back?
Shall the mistress work your slippers?
   Shall the master catch you flies?
Will you wear the mistress's watch?
   And the master's best white ties?

O Ranger! do just what you choose;
  Old friend, so gallant and dear;
What churl would dare refuse
  To drink your health with a cheer?
Old friend, in love and honour,
  Your name shall be handed down,
And children's hearts shall beat
  At the tale of your renown.

TWO BOYS.

Two boys stood on a height
    Reading their coming lives in earth
      and sky;
One clapp'd his hands in gay delight,
    And cried, " How grand a sailor-king
      am I!"
The other did not even *see* the waves
    That beat against the cliff in harmless
      strife;

I think he thought the world was only
    graves,—
    I think he thought the skies were
    only life.

One cried, " How grand a king!
    For I shall hold the storm-wind in
    my hand;
Shall crush the storm-beasts as they
    spring,
    And battle with the waves,—Ah, ha!
    how grand!
I on my deck am mighty lord of all,
    A monarch must obey my lightest
    breath,   [let fall
Each sign I give—each word that I
    Are to a hundred creatures life or
    death!"

" Oh, life !" the other cried ;
   Oh, death ! what are they ? death is
     life alone,
And if the tempest drown thy pride,
   And if thy word brings death, life is
     unknown ;
From me shall spring the only life in
     life.
   The only life in death; *let* tempests
     fall—
Let dreadful storm-beasts crush us in
     the strife,
   The death they bring, brings life,
     best life of all !"

"A BIRD IN THE HAND IS WORTH TWO IN THE BUSH."

In the hand—fluttering fearfully—
    Lonely and helpless,— poor little
        thing !
In the bush—peeping out cheerfully,
    Two together, gaily they sing !
Why is it best to have one in the hand ?
    Father, tell me,—I don't understand.

" Best it is because you have hold of
        it ;
    Child, it is only a figure of speech ;
Sunset shines, you look at the gold of
        it,
        Knowing well it is out of your
            reach ;
But the sixpence your godmother
        gave,
    Yours it is, to spend or to save."

Ah, that sixpence ! already I've done
        with it ;
    Never a penny with me will stay.
If I could buy but an inch of the sun
        with it,
    I might look at it every day.

Father, the birds shall stay in their
 nest !
Things that we never can have are
 best.

A CHILD'S FANCY.

O LITTLE flowers, you love me so,
   You could not do without me;
O little birds that come and go,
   You sing sweet songs about me;
O little moss, observed by few,
   That round the tree is creeping,
You like my head to rest on you,
   When I am idly sleeping.

O rushes by the river side,
　You bow when I come near you;
O fish, you leap about with pride,
　Because you think I hear you;
O river, you shine clear and bright,
　To tempt me to look in you;
O water-lilies, pure and white,
　You hope that I shall win you.

O pretty things, you love me so,
　I see I must not leave you;
You'd find it very dull, I know,—
　I should not like to grieve you.
Don't wrinkle up, you silly moss;
　My flowers, you need not shiver;
My little buds, don't look so cross;
　Don't talk so loud, my river.

I'm *telling* you I will not go,
    It's foolish to feel slighted;
It's rude to interrupt me so,
    You ought to be delighted.
Ah! now you're growing good, I see,
    Though anger is beguiling:
The pretty blossoms nod at me,
    I see a robin smiling.

And I will make a promise, dears,
    That will content you, maybe:
I'll love you through the happy years,
    Till I'm a nice old lady!
True love (like yours and mine) they say
    Can never think of ceasing,
But year by year, and day by day,
    Keeps steadily increasing.

FAIRY FACTS

THE KING'S BEARD.

IT is very tiresome when
    Fairies take dislike to kings.
I have known it now and then
    Lead to most unpleasant things.
I have even heard it said
Kings have wish'd that they were dead,
And I fancy it was so
With the King of Waggabo.

In the Waggabonian court
  There is worry and dismay,
For the king is growing short—
  Shorter—shorter—ev'ry day.
And it is a great distress
When a king grows less and less,
Lest the process should not stop
Till at last he goes off, pop.

Such a stately king was he,
  Very stout and very strong,
In his stockings six feet three,
  With a beard twelve inches long.
And the strangest part of all
Is, as he becomes less tall,
That the beard beneath his nose
Longer and yet longer grows.

Razors could not check or trim
  This strange growth, as it appear'd
Ev'ry inch that went from him
  Seem'd to settle in his beard.
Monday he was measured, when
His full height was five feet ten,
And on Friday, sad, but true,
He was barely three feet two.

And the courtiers soon begin
  Grumbling that no more he can
Seem a man with bearded chin,
  But a beard that has a man.
And they say they did not swear
Fealty to a tuft of hair.
Dreadful words are mutter'd low.
Treason broods in Waggabo.

The Archbishop cries, " I'm off!"
  And the Premier disappear'd :
Neither cared to serve a dwarf,
  Or to bow before a beard.
All the generals-in-chief
Ran away in gloomy grief,
And the admirals retreat
Fleetly with the frighten'd fleet.

But the barber cried, " Forbear !
  Ev'ry evil brings its good ;
Such a king is very rare,
  Let us prize him as we should.
Such a lovely beard doth not
Fall to ev'ry monarch's lot,
Nor can ev'ry barber's hand
Such delightful work command."

Page 199

Then the brave king knock'd him down
   (Barbers cannot hold their own),
Seized his sceptre and his crown,
   Wearily climb'd up his throne.
And with sounding gong did call
His good Commons, one and all,
And his noble house of peers
(Who can hardly speak for tears).

He addrest them with a chirp
   (Of his manly voice bereft),
" No usurper shall usurp
   While an inch of me is left.
While an inch of me remains
Still this hand shall hold the reins.
Still this head shall wear the crown,
Though this beard may drag me down.

"I may dwindle—I may shrink—
    Yes—I see—I feel I do;
But i' faith I do not think
    That my courage dwindles too!
Giants may believe I fear,
Beardless boys may jest and jeer,
But methinks I'll let them know
Who is king in Waggabo.

"And if *barbers* dare to speak"
    (Here he glanced behind the throne,
Where the barber pale and meek
    Held his head with painful moan),
"And if barbers dare to say
But one word by night or day,
Why I think this arm has still
Strength to work its master's will."

Then the weeping barber crept
  Very sadly to the door.
But an aged marquis stept
  Foremost on the marble floor,
With sublimest dignity
Cried, " The trembling traitor, see
Shall the crouching caitiff go ?
Is *that* law in Waggabo ?"

All the nobles of the land
  With a noble ardour flush'd,
Foot to foot and hand to hand
  Down upon the barber rush'd,
Frighten'd him to mortal fits,
Crying, " Tear him into bits,
Fling the pieces, base and foul,
To the dogs that howl and prowl."

The king tried to nod his head,
  But could only wag his beard,
For above its flaming red
  Scarce a bit of face appear'd.
And he shrivell'd more and more
Than he ever had before,
Till there's nothing left of him
But a beard within a rim.

And the nobles stand at bay,
  Ready at a word to leap
Where the wretched barber lay
  Coil'd in a repugnant heap.
Gallant are their souls and true;
Bright the eyes those souls shine througn.
Types of a majestic race,—
Emblem he of all that's base.

Out spake little Septimus
   (One of seven earls was he) :
" Shall our king be bearded thus,
   Unavenged by you and me?
I will smash the barber's bones,
You shall crush him between stones ;
They shall tear him limb from limb,
And we *all* will bury him !"

Then the barber stood upright,
   (Worms can turn and barbers too,)
Telling them it was not right
   Things like *that* to plan to do !
They might smash him if they could,
They might crush him if they would,
They might tear him limb from limb,
But they SHOULD NOT bury him !

Here the barber took his stand,
　　(At some point all creatures do,)
And his gesture of command
　　Show'd them that he meant it too.
Then the nobles asked apart,
" *Who* will eat this barber's heart ⁚
Some one must, to save defeat :
Who the barber's heart will eat ?"

The old marquis show'd his tongue ;
　　" Indigestion is my bane ;
Little Septimus is young,
　　He might cut and come again."
When they turn'd to urge him on,
Little Septimus was gone ;
He had vanish'd through the door,
And was never heard of more.

Dire confusion's everywhere!
　　Terrible are sight and sound!
Eyes are fix'd in ghastly stare,
　　And wild words ring wildly round!
Sentences are heard in part,
" Who will eat the barber's heart?"
Or in accents firm and free,
" They shall *never* bury me!"

From the hapless monarch's throne
　　Came a sort of twittering :—
" Take this beard, it is your own,—
　　All that's left you of your king!
Take me as a sacrifice
To appease the angry skies.
Burn me, and, for aught we know,
Peace will reign in Waggabo!"

He has spoken! words of awe!
  But the barber is inspired,
And pronounces it a law
  To do all the king desired.
Lest the lovely thing should spoil,
He anointeth it with oil,
And in tender solemn hush
Dresseth it with comb and brush.

Lays it out upon the ground,—
  What a laying out is that!
While the nobles kneel around,
  Every one without his hat.
From a box that's called Dispatch,
The old marquis takes a match;
To the barber, on the sly,
Hands it with averted eye.

And the match went phizzy phiz,
 As it makes its lurid glare,
And the beard goes phizzy phiz,
 With a smell of burning hair.
Playfully the bright flame whirls
Round those royal auburn curls—
Curls that deck'd a monarch's chin
Burning for a barber's sin.

  * * * * * *

Fairies softly whisp'ring are
 Close together in a rose :—
" If we carry this too far,
 What will happen no one knows !
Shall we end this foolish strife ?
Shall we save this monarch's life ?
Shall we change—of course we can,
Burning beard to living man ?''

'Tis no sooner said than done,
  (Words are many, acts are few),
Fairies like a bit of fun,
  But they are good-natured too!
From the ashes of the beard
That good king his form uprear'd;
Stately fellow, stout and strong,
With a beard twelve inches long!

Cheers ascended to the roof,
  Echoed back from ev'ry nook,
But the barber stood aloof,
  With a sort of hangdog look;
When the king sa'd, with a start,
" *Have* they ate the barber's heart?"
Off he sneak'd (as cowards can),
Let us hope a better man!

MORAL.

At the moral of this song
  Let no foolish fellow scoff;
If your beard is thought too long,
  You had better cut it off.
What the barber typifies
Is so plain to honest eyes,
That its meaning to define
Never shall be act of mine.

LORD RUBADUB.

'NEATH the shade of a daisy, just two
    inches high,
  A poor little fairy sits weeping alone;
She says, "What a desolate creature
    am I,
  My Lord Rubadub has the heart of a
    stone!

" He will not allow me to dance on a
　　cherry,
　　To swing in a cobweb, or ride on a
　　bee;
He tells me to *hush* when I want to be
　　merry,
　　Which is hard on a gay little fairy
　　like me.

" Our queen is so delicate, dainty, and
　　dear,
　　But I fear she will marry my Lord
　　Rubadub.
He struts at her side with a lounge and
　　a leer,—
　　I wonder she'll *look* at the dandified
　　cub !

" To fly from the court I announced my
    intention,
    But Rubadub says (and I fancy 'tis
       true),
I must serve seven years, or I'll not get
    my pension ;
    So what is a poor little fairy to
    do?

" Lord Rubadub's head is as large as
    my house ;
    His legs stride as far as the north
    from the south ;
He can hold in his hand that big
    monster, the mouse ;
    And he puts a whole dinner at once
    in his mouth !

" I do not deny he has wit and acu-
 men,
 But he's dreadfully fat and disgrace-
  fully tall;
I think he's a changeling, a thing they
 call human;
 I do not believe he's a fairy at all!

" But, hush! here he comes." So she
 hid in the moss,
 While vulgarly saunter'd, in insolent
  pride,
A fat little boy, who appear'd rather
 cross,
 Though the beautiful fairy queen flew
  at his side.

He flung himself down with a flop on
    the daisy,
    And sticking a meerschaum his thick
        lips between,
Bawl'd out, " Look alive there—Flare
    up—Don't be lazy,
    But fan me to sleep with your wings,
        fairy queen !"

The delicate fairy queen perch'd on his
    nose,
    And flapping her gossamer wings up
        and down,
The cross little fellow is wrapt in re-
    pose—
    A sneer on his lips, on his forehead a
        frown.

The delicate fairy queen falters and
    flutters,
    Afraid to desist. Ah, what slavery
      this !
But the fairy that's hid in the moss
    slily mutters,
    " Now, now is the moment to test
      WHAT HE IS !"

She creepeth along, (we can all guess
    what for,
    For who is so stupid as not to have
      heard
That test of a fairy, that signal of awe,
    That almost unspeakable, horrible
      word !)

She creepeth along, coming nearer and
    nearer;
  She reacheth one ear (for the crea-
    ture has two!)
Then shouts, and no bell than her voice
    sounded clearer,
  That almost unspeakable word, "Bug-
    aboo!"

Hey presto, he's gone! Down, down on
    the grass
  Drops the queen from the wonderful
    height of his nose.
Was he here? has he vanish'd? did
    none see him pass?
  Hey presto, he's gone! but *how*, no-
    body knows!

The sly little creature laughs out in de-
  rision;
    The queen's tears would soon float a
    fine fairy fish.
Then clapping their hands, they exert
  fairy vision;
    And flapping their wings, they see all
    that they wish.

They see a big chamber, in whose
  boundless space
    Sit fifty big boys, with big books in
    their hands,
And, lo! in the centre, in dreadful dis-
  grace,
    On a high stool of penance, Lord
    Rubadub stands.

Oh, fairy queen, faint not! that brow
    which thy kisses
  So often have touch'd, like the wing
    of a fly,
Is crown'd with a fool's cap of paper,
    where *this* is
  Engraved in black letters a hundred
    feet high :—

Tom the Truant, that's all; Tom
    the Truant—alas!
  Oh, fairy queen, weep, for thy darling
    they snub!
Oh, weep that such glory so lightly
    should pass,
  To find a cow'd schoolboy in Lord
    Rubadub!

The fairies are sorry,—they surely have
    reason;
  To see him stand there makes their
    tender hearts ache;
And their queen wore half-mourning
    for many a season,
  And rode a blackbeetle for Ruba-
    dub's sake.

THE WOUNDED DAISY.

At twilight in beautiful summers,
  When all the dew is shed,
And all the singers and hummers
  Are safe at home in bed,
In many a nook of the meadows
  Fairies may linger and lurk;
Look under the low grass-shadows,
  Perhaps you'll see them at work.

Perhaps you'll see them swinging
   On see-saw reeds in the dells;
Perhaps you'll hear them ringing
   The sweet little heather-bells;
Or setting the lilies steady,
   Before they begin to grow;
Or getting the rosebuds ready
   Before it is time to blow.

A fairy was mending a daisy
   Which some one had torn in half;
Her sisters all thought her crazy,
   And only looked on to laugh.
They showed her scores in the hedges,
   And scores that grew by the tarn,
And scores on the green field-edges,
   But she went on with her darn.

Then round they cluster, and chatter—
   How each had a flower more fine ;
One shook buttercups at her,
   And one brought briony-twine,
Strong red poppies to vex her,
   Tiny bright-eyes to beguile,
Tall green flags to perplex her ;
   But she worked on all the while.

She work'd and she sang this ditty,
   While insects wonder'd and heard
(They knew by the tone of pity
   The song was not from a bird),
" Daisy, somebody hurt you !
   Are you frighten'd at me ?
Patient hope is a virtue,
   Wait and you shall see !

" Was it a careless mower
 Cut your blossom in twain ?
I hope his hand will be slower
 When he sees you again.
Was it a step unheeding ?
 Or was it a stormy gale ?
Or was it—(*how* you are bleeding !)
 A dark malicious snail ?

" They did not know you would suffer,
 I think they had never seen ;
Slugs and snails may be rougher,
 Perhaps, than they always mean.
Do I not hear one sobbing,
 Down just there at my foot ?
Or is it only the throbbing
 Down in your poor little root ?

" Daisy, you were so merry
　　Where you modestly grew ;
Earth was generous, very,
　　Heaven was pleasant for you ;
Never teasing your neighbour,
　　Neither forward nor slack,—
Do you feel as I labour
　　Some of your joy come back

" Ah, you tremble a little !
　　Have I hurt you at last ?
If you were not so brittle,
　　I could mend you so fast.
No, there's nothing distressful,
　　Only a quiver of bliss,—
Daisy, I've been successful !
　　Grow, and give me a kiss !

" Now I've mended you neatly,
    All the fairies can see;
Now you look at me sweetly,
    Are you grateful to me?
I'll go hiding behind you,
    Then in a day or two,
Perhaps a baby will find you,
    And I shall hear it coo.

" Yes, your cheeks may be whiter
    Than the rest of your race;
Other eyes may be brighter,
    Others fairer in face;
But no flower that uncloses
    Can be precious as you,
Not an army of roses
    Fighting all the year through!"

Q

Then the fairies confess it,
    As that daisy revives;
All come round and caress it,
    All so glad that it lives.
No one ventures to doubt it,
    Hosts of penitent fays
Make their dance-rings about it,
    Sing their songs in its praise.

Years of fading and growing
    Pass,—the daisy is not!
Sweeter grass-blooms are growing
    Still by that little spot.
There each fairy that hover'd
    Sang while pausing above,
" Here the daisy recover'd,—
    Here's a footprint of Love !"

TRIAL BY JURY.

THE fairies have lost a fairy,
  They don't know what to do;
The rumours about her vary,
  And all of them can't be true.
They say she stood on a lily,
  And fell in its depths immense;
But I don't think she'd be so silly,
  For she was a fairy of sense!

They say that a butterfly riding,
   She dropp'd from a fearful height;
But her flymanship she took pride in,
   So I don't believe it quite.
They say they actually saw her
   Drown'd in a drop of rain;
They say an emmet came for her,
   Who won't bring her back again!

They cry, " Let us have a trial,
   A judge and a jury both,
And we will not accept a denial,
   And we'll all of us take an oath.
Of course, we're not wanting to hurt
   The troublesome little thing;   [her,
But when she is proved a deserter,
   We'll brand a big D on her wing."

So off they fly to a laurel
    That spread out its branches far,
And straightway begin to quarrel;
    How foolish fairies are!
They all refuse to be jury,
    They all desire to be judge;
They all strut about in a fury,
    Each owing the others a grudge.

Then little Snowbud, who ever
    Had something refined to say,
Remarks that the Major is clever,
    And some of his hair is grey.
But Wicksy exclaims, " I'll wager
    (Wicksy was never polite)
" The Captain's as 'cute as the Major,
    And most of *his* hair is *white!*"

The Major runs forward bowing,
　　And pushing his bright hair back;
They all clap their hands, avowing
　　That grey grows under the black.
The Captain sits down despairing,
　　" Fool that I was!" he cries;
" This morning I dyed my hair in
　　Solution of Bluebottle flies!"

They take the respectable Major,
　　Pluck some of the black hairs out,
Cut off the rest with a razor,
　　And frizz the grey locks about.
They wrap a thick cobweb o'er him,
　　His eyebrows they fiercely smudge,
They kneel in the dust before him,
　　And call him a lovely judge.

They seize upon twelve old fairies,
   So old they can hardly fly;
They say, " Never mind what your hair
   Our jury you'll be or—die!"   [is,
The old fairies crouch and shiver,
   And cry it is most unfair;
But the Judge just points to the river,
   And says, "We have sacks—beware!"

So every one is pleasant,
   As if no cloud had been:
The jury is quite quiescent,
   The judge is all serene.
The only drawback I heard of
   (And that was but by the bye)
Was just that there was not a word of
   Any pris'ner to try.

So the judge put on his black cap
    In a death-condemning speech,
Which the jury declared was clap-trap,
    And begg'd him not to preach.
The jury said, " Guilty, 'pon honour,"
    While loudly cheer'd the crowd;
The judge pronounced sentence on her,
    And the Captain swore aloud.

Thus, the trial being ended,
    They all began to dance,
And Wicksy his steps defended
    As just come over from France.
Then some of them took to kissing,
    And loudly for supper did call,   [ing
Where the fairy they thought was miss-
    Gobbled up more than them all.

THE FOX.

Two children are lost in a wood,
   What can they do ? what can they do ?
They have not a morsel of food,
   And nothing to drink but dew !
Looking to earth and to skies,
   All that they saw, all that they saw,
Only increased their surprise,
   And only heighten'd their awe.

A squirrel peep'd out of his bed,
   Up in a tree, up in a tree.
" Poor little beggars," he said,
   " How you must wish you were me !
Look at my warm little tail,
   Fur tippet too, fur tippet too ;
Squirrels can never turn pale,
   Poor little shavers, like you !"

Birds, tuck'd up snug in their nests,
   Nodded their heads, nodded their
     heads ;
Muffled their wings and their breasts,
   Order'd them off to their beds.
Rabbits ran out of their holes,
   Crying " For shame," crying " For
     shame,

To wake up respectable souls !
　What is your business or claim ?"

A fox looking sly (as it sat,—
　Who says it can't? who says it can't?)
Wink'd like a wide-awake man
　Trying to do a rich aunt ;
Wink'd like a wide-awake " cove"
　Hiding his jokes, hiding his jokes ;
Whispering, " Trust to my love,
　I'll help you, sweet little folks."

The children went up to him straight :
　" Dear Mr. Fox, dear Mr. Fox,
Please take us home to the gate
　That opens if any one knocks.

Nurse will run out in a trice;
    Towser won't bite, Towser won't bite;
Cook will prepare something nice;
    Mammy will laugh with delight."

"Done," cried the Fox, "and why not?
    Each take an arm, each take an
        arm;
Let us proceed at a trot,
    Mental emotions to charm.
I know the way, if you please,—
    No one so well, no one so well;
Here by the sycamore-trees,
    There, through the buttercup dell."

Children, his flatteries shun!
    He is no friend, he is no friend.

Page 236

They who with foxes do run
   Always look small in the end!
Honey'd his phrases and looks;
   Sweetly he mocks, sweetly he mocks;
Have you not read in your books
   Words saying " Sly as a fox"?

Who ever heeded advice?
   No one *I* know, no one *I* know.
The children declare he is nice,
   And doubting a fellow is low.
Easy it is to abuse;
   Ill-nature shocks, ill-nature shocks;
We can confide where we choose;
   They'll put their faith in the fox!

Blind, inconsiderate, rash!
   Rush on your fate, rush on your fate.

He who trusts foxes goes smash,
  As you'll discover too late !
Gaily the trio proceed,
  Still arm-in-arm, still arm-in-arm.
Foxes not trusty, indeed !
  Innocent foxes do harm !

" Here is your own pretty park ;
  Come through the grass, come
    through the grass.
Hark to the supper-bell, hark !
  Now through this thicket we'll
    pass,—
Pass through this beautiful glade ;
  Dancing with joy, dancing with joy.
Put your foot *here*, little maid ;
  Put yours down *there*, darling boy."

Oh, what two horrible screams!
  (Poor little toes, poor little toes).
Nightmares that neigh in their dreams
  Utter such sounds, I suppose.
Two traps are set on two slides,
  Foxes to snare, foxes to snare;
Reynard is holding his sides
  At the two children caught there.

Taking his hat off, he bows
  Very polite, very polite :—
" 'Tis your papa that allows
  These little gimcracks to bite;
By your most worshipful pa'
  Set for the brute, set for the brute;
You've put your foot in it—ha!
  I've got the length of your foot!"

Fairies were dancing about,
   Close to the gin, close to the gin ;
Saw that sly Reynard was out,
   Saw that the children were in.
" Stop him, we won't let him run."
   Eager they spoke, eager they spoke:
" Foxes don't understand fun,—
   Ill-nature spoils the best joke !"

Ten fairies seize on each leg,—
   Call him their own, call him their own ;
Reynard doth abjectly beg
   That they will let him alone !
Children jump out at their touch,
   Happy and free, happy and free ;
Reynard remarks 'tis too much,
   For they're no better than he.

But the immovable fays
　　Tumble him in, tumble him in;
Bid him repent of his ways,
　　In the delectable gin.
Slyboots, your boots pinch you now?
　　Rather too tight? rather too tight?
Very good lodgings, I vow;
　　Purchased by very poor spite!

MORAL.

To Children.

Shame, disappointment, and care,
　　Bruises and knocks, bruises and
　　　knocks,
Such is their portion who dare
　　Walk arm-in-arm with a fox.

R

To Foxes.

Foxes, who deal in sly blows,
    Pause, if you please, pause, if you
      please;
Trying to pinch other toes,
    May not your own get a squeeze?

PATS OF BUTTER.

FAIRIES can hide anywhere,
   Up and down, and in and out,
'Neath the cushion of a chair,
   In a teapot's empty spout;
They can nestle in your hair,
   They can creep beneath your chin;
Fairies can hide anywhere,
   Up and down, and out and in.

Fairies are so very small,
   That I think we cannot be
Ever safe from them at all,
   On the earth or on the sea;
For we are so big and tall,
   And our eyes so powerful are—
Fairies being very small,
   Are beyond our vision far.

Fairies are so full of tricks:
   I have heard the farmers say,
They have stolen from the ricks
   All the blossoms of the hay;
And with little dabs and pricks
   Made the horses plunge and rear,—
Fairies are so full of tricks,
   So extremely odd and queer!

In the dairy stood the cream,
    Fresher than the snowflake white,
And the butter that a dream
    Never churn'd more sweetly bright :
'Neath the moon's delightful beam,
    On a summer evening fair,
In the dairy stood the cream,
    And a fairy spied it there.

And a fairy spied it,—that
    Tells the story, does it not ?
They may whip the patient cat,
    Who the sweet cream never got.
At the door poor Pussy sat,
    Sorrowfully mew'd and purr'd ;
But a fairy spied it,—*that*
    Tells the story in a word !

She was hidden by a fly
  On the dairy-floor that slept;
When the moon was in the sky,
  From beneath its wing she stept.
Greedy creature, brisk and sly,
  With a flourish and a hop,
Spurns the carcase of the fly,
  Drains the sweet cream ev'ry drop.

Tipsy with the luscious draught,
  Little tumbling, reeling thing,
How she coo'd and how she laugh'd,
  Toss'd her head and plumed her wing;
But the liquor that she quaff'd
  Rapidly revenge can take;
She was tipsy with the draught,
  And her head began to ache!

Fairies are cut up so soon,
   Such a little makes them mope;
If a gnat sings out of tune,
   I have known them give up hope;
I have seen them croak and croon
   If a dewdrop touch'd their wings—
Fairies are cut up so soon,
   Are such nervous little things!

Where the lovely butter lies,
   She betakes her to repose;
Closeth little tipsy eyes,
   Cooleth little blushing nose,
Sinking, to her great surprise,
   Deeper, deeper in the cup;
Where the lovely butter lies,
   Is a fairy swallow'd up!

In the morning Susan comes,
    Scolds the most misjudged of cats,
" Flaxen-headed Ploughboy" hums
    While she forms the butter pats ;
Active fingers, willing thumbs
    Knead them into pretty shape.
In the morning Susan comes,—
    Captive fairy can't escape.

Happy faces welcome are
    Where the pleasant breakfast is:
This is oldest grandpapa,
    Youngest little grandchild this ;
Children running from afar,
    Sons and daughters not a few,
At the table welcome are,—
    So is bread and butter too.

Greedy Jim is always rude,
   Pokes his hand in every dish ;
In his hurry to intrude,
   Swallows bones instead of fish ;
Swallows bad instead of good ;
   Snatches meat, but swallows fat,—
Greedy Jim, extremely rude,
   Swallows a whole butter-pat !

" Goodness ! Jim, don't look so wild !"
   " Gracious ! Jim, don't scream so shrill !"
" What's the matter with the child ?"
   " Goodness, gracious ! are you ill ?"
Father's getting rather riled,
   Mother hardly draws her breath,—
" Goodness ! Jim, don't look so wild ;
   Sure you frighten us to death !"

Tumbling down and leaping up,
　　Twisting limbs in ev'ry shape ;
Rolling, grov'lling like a pup,
　　Mowing, mopping like an ape ;
Tasting neither bit nor sup,—
　　Yelling like an imp in pain ;
Tumbling down and leaping up,—
　　Certainly the boy's insane.

Little have his parents guess'd
　　Whence the mighty mischief springs ;
Men and women, much depress'd,
　　Recommend a hundred things.
But it's hard, if truth's confess'd,
　　To find cure or antidote ;
For—a fairy in your chest,
　　Trying to ascend your throat !

All unchanged by day and night,
   All unchanged by night and day,
Desperately showing fight,
   Conqueror in ev'ry fray.
Eyes are weary of the sight,
   Ears are deafen'd by the roar;
All unchanged by day and night,
   Till the weeks were number'd four.

Then a mouse, in mere disgust,
   (Sensible, though very small,)
Murmur'd it was most unjust
   That he could not sleep at all;
Gnaw'd the wainscot into dust,
   The apartment enter'd in,
And, in absolute disgust,
   Made a spring at Jimmy's chin!

Took possession of his tongue,
  Saying, with disdainful squeak,
" Come, my lad, you are but young,
  Let your betters act and speak !"
Then his little forelegs flung
  Down the throat of Master Jim,
Backing nimbly on his tongue,
  Dragg'd the fairy out of him !

MORAL.

Butter-pats, to eat alone,
  Is a crime the wise forbid ;
Naughty children must atone
  For their sins, as Jimmy did.
Fairies should drink mountain dew,—
  Cream's too dear at any price ;
And if danger threatens you,
  Always put your trust in mice.

A SLIGHT CONFUSION.

"WHAT's the use of fairies?" said the
    child,
  "What's the use of fairies at all?
The weeds in my garden grow wild,
    And I've lost my favourite ball;
My poor little bird is dead,
    They won't let me milk the cow,
And this lesson will never be said,
    For I ought to be learning it now!

" If fairies were *like* fairies, you know,
   Of the least bit of use or good,
The weeds would just die as they grow,
   And my ball jump out of the wood;
My birdie would live again,
   I'd find the cow in my bed,
And this lesson that gives me such pain,
   Would grow of itself in my head."

So she sat down on the floor to cry,
   The dear little sensible thing !
And the fairies made no reply,
   Not even so much as to sing !
She heard a moo as she sat,—
   A moo, I say, not a mia-u,
And she cried, " Why that *is* not the cat,
   But it never can be the cow !"

The door flew open with *such* a bang,
  And the cow came careering through,
The pail on her bright horns she swang,
  " Milk me quickly," she cried ; " pray
    do !"
The child stood up in amaze,
  And said, with a timid laugh,
" Well, surely, of all the queer plays,
  This play is the queerest by half!"

But the cow kept running round and
    round,
  Like a cow that was quite distraught,
And she mooed with a dreadful sound,
  No moo that her poor mother taught.
The child sprang up on a chair,
  Crying, " Oh, cow, please don't !"

But the cow career'd through the air,
 Replying, " Is it likely I won't ?"

At that moment the poor little bird,
 That was lying dead in its cage,
Call'd out, "You're enough, on my word,
 To put a dead bird in a rage!"
The weeds in her garden knock'd
 On the window, they'd grown so tall,
And laugh'd when they saw she look'd
  shock'd,
 And she thought *that* the worst of all !

Then the grammar she held in her hand
 Dropp'd down on the floor with a jar,
And she murmur'd, "I don't understand ;
 How troublesome all the things are !"

She rubb'd her eyes, and she said,
　As she took a frighten'd peep,
"The cow's not here, and the bird is
　　dead,
　And I fancy I've been asleep!"

And a fairy, all beauty and light,
　Reproachfully perch'd on her ear,
And gave it a sharp little bite,
　Till she scream'd out with pain and fear.
But the fairy cried, "Alas!
　Why didst thou utter abuse?
The world has come to a pretty pass,
　When fairies are called of no use!

"Little girl, thou must thy part fulfil,
　If we're to take kindly to ours:

s

Then pull up the weeds with a will,
  And fairies will cherish the flowers;
Feed thy poor prisoner, the bird,
  Or fairies its spirit will free;
Learn of thy lesson each difficult word,
  And fairies will smile upon thee."

Said the child, "I don't understand,
    quite,
  There surely is something forgot,—
Are fairies permitted to bite?
  Or is it a dream, or what?
What is the moral? and why?
  The cow alone should be blamed—
The fairy takes ground extremely high,
  But I don't feel a bit ashamed!"

THE WEDDING-RING.

PART I.

CHILDREN should not leave about
  Anything that's small and bright,
Lest the fairies spy it out,
  And fly off with it at night.
Foolish people wonder so
Where the little pins can go
  That are lost through years and years
Surely every one must know
  Fairies take them for their spears!

Even scissors, knives, and rings,
  Though so large, and such a weight,
(Little avaricious things,
  So ambitious to be great!),
I have known them steal away,
As the ants do sticks and clay
  (For united strength is strong);
You may see ants every day,
  Dragging heavy weights along.

Through the bright grass fluttering,
  Laughing till they cannot speak,
Moonlight fairies softly spring,
  Playing games of Hide and Seek.
And a little blue-eyed fay,
Deftly hides herself away
  From the eager-seeking troop,

Calling out in accent gay
  Such a pretty fairy " whoop !"

Hunting low and hunting high,
  Whispering and shouting loud ;
" Chaffing " her for being shy,
  Mocking her for being proud.
Spreading o'er the moonlit sands,
All dispersed in shining bands ;
  Searching still—and still at fault,—
Till a fairy claps her hands,
  And proclaims a sudden halt.

Lo, she points her tiny foot,
  Silent in her great surprise,
Where beside a primrose root,
  Such a dazzling creature lies ;

Eager fairies round it come,
Pompous fairies haw and hum,
  Timid fairies shrink in fright;
Can it talk, or is it dumb?
  Will it hurt us? can it bite?

Then the wisest fairy born
  (Almost thought too wise to thrive)
Touch'd it with a sort of scorn,
  Saying, " It is not alive;"
Saying, " 'Tis a golden thing;"
Saying, " 'Tis a wedding-ring.
  Wedding-ring for mortal made,
Bitter grief its loss will bring
  To the Princess Scherazade!"

Azurine, the blue-eyed fay,
  Who had hid herself erewhile,

Join'd them in a sulky way,
  Pouting lips that ought to smile.
Angry that the sport forsook,
They forgot for her to look;
  So she said, extremely cross,
" Let us throw it in the brook,
  Careless losers merit loss!"

But Luline cried, " Not so,
  Let us neither lose nor keep;
Unkind fairies—don't you know?—
  Find it hard to go to sleep;
For a little conscience pricks
Worse than little thorns in sticks.
  But a little heart at ease
Better is than pranks or tricks;
  Let us be good fairies, please!"

They divided into parts,
   All according to their lights;
Luline led the Tender Hearts,
   Azurine the Tricksy Sprites.
Wise Monimia lonely stood,
Would not join with bad or good,
   So abuse from both did get.
(Well, I really never could
   See the use of wisdom yet!)

Tricksy Sprites have seized the ring,
   But Luline cries, " How unfair!
Muster, Tender Hearts, and spring
   On the robbers gather'd there!
Azurine, just turn about,
You and I should fight it out.
   Single combat is the dodge.

Don't engage the rabble rout
  In a horrible hodge-podge!"

Azurine laugh'd saucily.
  "I have got it, you have not.
This is well from you to me,
  Who have not what I have got!
Come, my gay, successful troop,
Roll it, 'tis a golden hoop.
  Hoop is a delicious play;
Let the conquer'd mourn and droop,
  Every fairy has her day!"

As the golden creature flew
  Swifter than the feather'd dart,
What did little Luline do—
  Luline of the tender heart?

Noble spirit—nerves high-strung,
Through the hoop HERSELF she flung,
  Stopping the too dreadful race,
And, while cheers of rapture rung,
  Lay exhausted on her face !

It was by the river's side,
  Moment more had been too late ;
In the darkly-flowing tide
  Wedding-ring had met its fate ;
Azurine cried, " Hip, hurrah !
Tender Hearts the victors are ;
  Luline is the queen of queens.
Luline of the tender heart,
What a thorough brick thou art,
  Worth a thousand Azurines !"

Then the noble foes embrace,
　　As brave foes have done before;
Hand to hand and face to face,
　　Hug each other more and more.
All in pleased contentment gaze;
Then the wedding-ring they raise,
　　Polish it from stain or speck,
And, with little songs of praise,
　　Hang it round Lulina's neck!

PART II.

In the night she cannot sleep
　　For the depth of her distress;

In the day she can but weep—
   Lovely, sorrowful princess!
On her hand she draws her glove
At the footstep of her love,
   Of her love, the royal prince;
Trembling like a frighten'd dove,
   At his touch she seems to wince.

Dared she but her grief to tell
   To the prince who loved her so,
Then, perchance, had all been well,
   Though indeed we cannot know;
For she had not strength for that,
And her heart went pit-a-pat
   At the notion of the thing.
So in misery she sat
   Mourning for her wedding-ring.

For Prince Azof swore one night
That her white hands should not be
Always cover'd from the sight,
But that all who liked should see;
For no hands were ever known
White and lovely as her own;
And no jewel should she wear,
But her wedding-ring alone
Should enclasp one finger fair.

And the hour is very near,
And the banquet rich is spread,
When she knows she must appear
With her hands uncover̀ed.
How she wrings them in her grief!
Crying out for some relief—
Crying out in her distress,

" I of mourners am the chief,
  Most unfortunate princèss!"

What is that which floateth by,
  Scarcely seen and scarcely heard?
Little shining butterfly?
  Little radiant humming-bird?
Doth it brush her brow and cheek?
Will it sing or will it speak?
  Doth it glitter, glance, and gleam?
Will it melt like snow-crown'd peak?
  Is it real or a dream?

It is gone,—but in her hand
  (Ah, what joy a sunbeam brings!)
Lies that precious marriage band,
  Most beloved of wedding-rings!

On her finger soon shines bright
That small rim of golden light,
   Which she welcomes with a kiss,
Cooing out her soft delight
   At a happy chance like this.

THE LITTLE WHITE DOE.

In the beautiful forest is straying
   An innocent little white doe,
And the creature is happily playing
   With the sunlight that flickereth so ;
The sunlight so soft and so tender,
   That moves with each leaf as it moves,
And the doe, quite amazed at its splen-
    dour,
   Is hunting the beam that she loves !

Alas! is she never reflecting
　　How far she has roamed from the
　　　track?
How far from the mother expecting
　　Her darling who does not come back?
Alas! can the sunshine deceive her?
　　The sunshine so tender and bright;
Can it lure her from home, and then
　　　leave her
　　Alone in the darkness of night?

Dark night round the forest is closing,
　　It frightens the little white doe,
Who earnestly longs to be dozing
　　With the mother that fondles her so.
The cold makes the little thing shiver,
　　She bleats for the sunshine that's fled,

T

She lays herself down by the river,
   And mournfully thinks she is dead.

By the side of that stream brightly flow-
     ing
   A dear little child has to pass;
To her home she is leisurely going,
   When she sees something white in
     the grass.
She cries out, with joy in each feature,
   " How charming a plaything is this !
You dear little beautiful creature,
   I hope you will give me a kiss !"

Quite close to her breast she doth fold it,
   And kisses its innocent face,
Her fat little arms can just hold it,
   And she walks with a tottering pace.

Her home by the bright fire is lighted,
   With triumph she opens the door,
She enters,—she laughs out delighted,
   And puts down the doe on the floor!

It moves not,—as motionless lying
   As if it was modell'd in snow;
It is pretty if dead or if dying,—
   It moves not,—ah, poor little doe!
Then May wrings her hands in her
     sorrow,
   And almost in anger she cries,—
" Are you dead? will you not live to-
     morrow,
   And open your beautiful eyes?

" In my arms, little doe, I will take
     you,

You freeze me, so cold have you
    grown,
But indeed I will never forsake you ;
    I found you, and you are my own."
With that white, frozen thing, sadly
    weeping,
    She mournfully creeps to her bed,
And clasps to her bosom while sleeping
    The doe she believes to be dead !

The heart of the dear little maiden
    Beats against the cold breast of the
    doe,
With love is that tender heart laden,
    And love works enchantment we
    know.
Yes, life through the creature is stealing,
    Her heart gives an answering beat,

Page 277

And the wonder she cannot help feeling
  Finds vent in a pitiful bleat !

May wakes, in the low sound delighting,
  Embraces the doe in her bed,
And feeds her with milk, so inviting
  'Twould almost give life to the dead.
She smoothes her soft hairs as a duty,
  She washes her free from each speck,
And a blue ribbon, bright in its beauty,
  She ties round her pretty white neck.

The doe is quite pleased with such pet-
    ting,
  And fondly keeps licking her hand,
But still in her heart is regretting
  Her home in the free forest land.

She utters a sorrowful bleating,
   But May comprehends not the strain,
For the meaning that sound is repeat-
     ing
   Is " Please take me back, dear, again."

One day in the forest they're playing,
   And frisking with frolicsome glee,
And further and further keep straying,
   Like creatures that love to be free.
Ah! oak, with thy branches wide spread-
     ing,
   Once dear to the doe's startled mind,
Ah! track to a happy home leading,
   She runs on and looks not behind.

She runs like the wind,—swiftly flying,
   She reaches the well-beloved glade,

And there her old mother is lying
   Asleep in the beautiful shade.
Through the long ferns her wee darling
     presses,
   Ah, softly she slackens her pace,
With tenderest bleats and caresses
   She crouches and licks her dear face.

Oh, rapturous, passionate meeting,
   Oh, moments that form a bright past,
Too exquisite not to be fleeting,
   Yet follow'd by joy that can last!
May watches them, tearful and breath-
     less,
   Her pleasure is mix'd with regret ;
She sees their affection is deathless,
   She feels she must part from her pet.

But after much talking and loving
   (Not a word of it May understands),
The mother towards her is moving,
   And rubs her soft nose in her hands.
And when,—for the stars are now peep-
     ing,—
   May runs o'er the dew-cover'd ground,
The old doe beside her is creeping
   And the young one is frisking around.

Quite close to May's cottage they made
     them
   A new home so pretty and neat;
Each night in that warm nest they laid
     them,
   Each morning waked May with their
     bleat.

The wee doe jumps up to caress her
  With kisses she prizes, we know,
And the mother's fond eyes softly bless
    her
  For her love to the Little White Doe!

THE BUTTERFLY AND THE FAIRIES.

A BUTTERFLY was grieved one day
Because he could do nought but play;
He envied bees and birds and ants,
And senseless stones and common plants,
And leaves that feed the life of trees,
And tiny builders in the seas,
And breathings of the summer gale,
That waft a seed or swell a sail,

And winter's fleece of folded snow,
That wraps the roots before they grow,
And light that wakes the hope of earth,
And shade that shelters every birth,
And dew that fosters every bloom,
And heat and silence and perfume,
All things were sent to toil and strive,
To keep this happy world alive :
No wonder tales and sermons grim
Pointed their morals oft at him,
For all had work to do, except
Himself—and here he paused and wept.

He flutter'd on through tracts of air,
So sorrowful, he knew not where,
Away from all that once he sought,
He cared not what the roses thought ;

A daring lily, full of dew,
Struck his swift bosom as he flew,
Great was the shock, but on he pass'd,
And on and up and far and fast,
Till scarcely fit to sit or stand,
He came at length to Fairyland.

A busy scene !   Laborious fays !
He watches them in mute amaze,
The whirr goes on from morn to night,
Some twisting threads of bloom and
        light ;
Some weaving each resplendent line,
Into a fabric soft and fine ;
Some cutting shapes with anxious care ;
Some ever sorting, pair by pair ;
Some bringing tiny moulds and prints,
To stamp the wares with rainbow tints ;

Some piling up the finish'd bales;
Some packing them in dockleaf mails,
Arranging, cording, ticketing—
" These for the realms of earth, next
      spring :"
In short, it was, as all might see,
A fairy manufactory.

Sadly he watch'd them while they
      wrought :
" Here too is toil," 'twas thus he thought,
In all the lustre of this clime,
Not even a sylph is wasting time,
All have their task to toil and strive,
To keep this happy world alive,
All have their work.   I wish I knew
What lovely business they do !

" It must be something great and grand
To need the skill of fairyland.
Queen Morning's robes of rich device,
She never wears the same dress twice!
I wonder if I've rightly guess'd,
I'll ask when next they stop to rest."

While thus he stood to see and hear,
A brisk light porter saunter'd near,
And touch'd his foxglove with an air
That ask'd him what he wanted there;
Had he an order?   It should be
Attended to immediately;
Or a complaint?   He might depend
On their endeavour to amend.
Perhaps a little bill to pay?
Or had he only lost his way?

" No," quoth the wanderer, " none of
     these ;
But, will you tell me, if you please,
What all these busy workers do ?"

" Why here's a lark ?   I thought you
     knew !"
(He utter'd with a knowing twang
That pretty phrase of fairy slang,
Made when a lark, benighted, found
Its wondering way to elfin ground,
And the small folk believed with awe,
It was a dragon that they saw.)
" Look round me, stranger—use your
     eyes ;
We make the *wings of butterflies.*"

" Oh, waste of labour, to adorn
A plaything, which the wise must
     scorn !
Toil rather for the bee, whose fame
I envy, though I must not claim,
And leave the useless butterfly,
Unmark'd to live, unmourn'd to
     die."

Shouts of fine laughter while he spoke
Betrayed how fairies love a joke;
(On earth the mothers mused that day,
What made their leaping babes so gay,
For well the darlings understand
When there is fun in fairyland.)
A hoary sylph his smiles suppress'd,
And gravely answer'd for the rest:

"Weep not," he said, "nor look
   askance
At thy most sweet inheritance;
Thou hast thy purpose; be content
To teach the use of ornament.
Honey, which human hearts can drink,
Is better than the bees', I think;
And though not stored in comb or
   hive,
It keeps this happy world alive.
The child who marks thy fluttering
   way,
And stops a moment in his play,
And feels at that familiar sight,
Some little movement of delight,—
Learns what no years of toil can teach,
Looks at the regions out of reach,

Sees some dim shadow of the Power
" Which vein'd the shell and shaped the
        flower ;
" And said to wisdom, work, and pelf,
" Beauty is precious for itself!"

OLD DONALD.

Up in the Highlands of Scotland
　　The fairies are very rude;
I do not know if all are so—
　　Some of them may be good.
But I will write you a story
　　Of the events of a night;
And as you read, you'll own, indeed,
　　The fairies were not polite.

A very old man was Donald,
   His cheeks were shrivell'd and lean;
His teeth were few, and broken, too,
   With very big gaps between.
He stoop'd his shoulders in walking,
   His head was uncrown'd by hair;
His beard was white, his legs a sight,
   For of calves they were quite bare.

He liked both snuff and tobacco,
   He wore an old-fashioned coat;
On whisky-punch at dinner or lunch
   He certainly seem'd to doat.
For he was an old campaigner;
   I've heard the young fellows say,
It was no joke with him to smoke,
   To drink, to fight, or to play.

One night at home he was setting
   His whisky-punch in a jug   [clay,
(For punch, they say, tastes best from
   As beer from a pewter mug);
He said, "I don't know the reason,
   But when I'm mixing this stuff,
I never find that, to my mind,
   I put in whisky enough!

"Perhaps I had better marry!
   Since women can make strong tea;
They'd surely brew this creature too,
   So as to satisfy me.
But there's the trouble of wooing;
   I never can quite make out,
If girls I meet in fair or street,
   What I should chatter about.

" I think I'll go out this evening,
   And to the first girl I see,
I'll simply say in a passing way,
   ' My dear, will you marry me?'
I'm a very handsome fellow,
   I've plenty of gold and gear;
'Twould be odd indeed if I can't succeed
   In bringing a woman here."

And oh, but Donald was cunning!
   The sly fox did not forget
The fairest maid in sun or shade
   Just then was sure to be met!
For down to the brook fair Peggy
   Did every evening go,
Her pitcher to fill at the sparkling rill,
   As cunning Donald did know.

Page 295

But the fairies heard him prating,
　　And laugh'd in their fairy sleeves;
His foolish talk they meant to balk,
　　For folly a fairy grieves.
Fair Peggy sits in her cottage,
　　Her pretty hands glance and gleam,
For she must sew another row
　　Before she runs to the stream.

Most haste is worst speed, fair Peggy,
　　And why do you work so quick?
A needle so fine can glance and shine,
　　But oh, it can also prick!
And when a determined fairy
　　Takes up his post at its head,
And pushes it into your tender skin,
　　Why, then, some blood will be shed.

Fair Peggy holds out her finger,
  And pain makes her knit her brow;
Her grandmother cried with an air of
    pride,
  "How clumsy the girls are now!
When *I* was young, hoity-toity!
  When pretty and young was I,
I was sonsy and sweet, and nimble and
    neat—"
  Here Peggy began to cry!

Her grandmother seized the pitcher,
  And grumbled on with her scold,
"Sure nobody cares how he worries
    and wears
  The bones that are very old!

And *I* must run to the river,
  Because you have prick'd your thumb.
Let people take care, and preachers be-
      ware,
  Or the world to an end will come!"

So off the old woman hobbled—
  (A very old woman she;)
She had a beard, and her eyes were
      blear'd,
  And so she could hardly see.
Her nose was like a potato,
  Her voice was crack'd and shrill,
Her head was bare for want of hair,
  And she liked to have her will!

And lo! she was met by Donald,
  Who raised his hat from his brow,

And look'd so sly, and wink'd his eye,
　And made a capital bow;
And cried, with a manly flourish,
　" My match you won't often see,
Or come or go? or yes or no?
　My dear, will you marry me?"

Now, Donald had lost his glasses;
　And was it that, do you think?
Or was it the spell by the fairy well?
　Or was it the power of drink?
He thought it was lovely Peggy
　Was standing there by the stream;
That maiden bright, who, many a night,
　Had mix'd his punch in his dream!

The grandmother dropp'd a curtsey
　As well as her stiff knees could;

She thought to herself, he has plenty of
  pelf,
  And rule him I surely could.
With wink to his wink replying,
  With look that was slyer still,
She answer'd his word as pert as a bird,
  " Indeed, my dear, and I will !"

Together they sought a blacksmith,—
  In Scotland it's known to all,
That man and wife are join'd for life
  By almost nothing at all !
It's rather a shaky business,
  And some it might not content;
But trouble's a bore, and perhaps to
  take more
  Brings its own punishment.

The blacksmith snigger'd a little,
　　But he wouldn't make a row,
So married them both by word and by
　　　oath
　　Before you could say bow-wow.
Says he, " If driving a tandem,
　　A better match who could pick ?"
" Sure, man alive ! it's *I* shall drive,"
　　The woman replied quite quick.

Now, was it the sudden feeling
　　Of being a married man ?
(If you're not a block, it's an awful
　　　shock;
　　Bear it as well as you can !)
Or had the fumes of the whisky
　　Floated away from his brain ?

Or fairies, for fun, their spell undone,
   And given him eyes again?

He saw it was Peggy's grandame,
   And not the sweet Peg herself,
Who, honest and fair, had married him
      there,
   And must brew the punch in his delf!
And if you believe you've married
   A beautiful village belle,
And find that instead you've her grand-
      mother wed,
   It re-al-ly *is* a sell!

The old woman smiled and simper'd,
   And feebly her head did wag,
Says she, " My love, we'd better move."
   Says he, " Avaunt, you hag!"

Says she " I'm a married woman—
  Your own respectable wife!"
Says he, " If so, for weal and woe,
  I'll plague you out of your life!"

Says she, " You are old and crabbed,
  But two can play at that game;
If you are cross, 'twill be *your* loss;
  I'm sure *I* can be the same!"
Says he, all flush'd with his passion,
  " I shall not mind you a bit!"
Says she, " I hear—be calm, my dear,
  Or, may be you'll have a fit!"

The fairies are laughing round them,
  They laugh till they cannot stand,
And then advance in a mocking dance—
  Oh, mischievous fairy band!

Oh, band of mischievous fairies
   That flicker and float about;
You've had your play,—do fly away,—
   You'll do no good, I doubt!

But up in the Scottish Highlands
   The fairies are very rude;
They've too much ' cheek,' and love to
      speak,
   And don't care how they intrude.
So they encourage the quarrel,
   Just for the sake of the game;
But to provoke, although in joke,
   I always think is a shame.

They all of them flock round Donald,
   To egg him on to the fight;

Thegrandmother *knew* (and isn't it true?)
   That women are always right!
So *she* needed no incentive;
   But Donald's not brisk at all: [fears,
They breathe in his ears their comical
   That shortly he'll sing rather small!

" *You* to be found chicken-hearted,
   After the whisky you've drunk!
You on the sly to eat humble pie!
   You to be put in a funk!
You to be done by a woman!
   You to be quizz'd by the men!
You to be beat! *you* to retreat!
   You to be peck'd by a hen!"

This is the song they are singing,
   (Fairies are certainly shrewd);

Thus they give tongue—isn't it wrong
   And most uncommonly rude?
Up in the Highlands of Scotland
   Manners are not what they were;
He that's ill-fed groweth ill-bred,
   So are the fairies up there!

Into the midst she comes tripping,
   Scatters her sunshine about,
Laughs like the skies, sings with her eye,
   Leads her old grandmother out.
Up in the Highlands of Scotland
   Maidens are bonnie and bright,
They can endure well to be poor;
   Courteous are hearts that are light.

Donald is sipping his whisky!
   Is it the very same tap?

x

What shall he do ? can it be true ?
    Has he waked up from a nap ?
Still floats the song of the fairies
    As the good toddy he stirr'd.
Does it not change ? that would be strange ;
    Is *this* the song he first heard ?

" Old men should mate with old women,
    Girls are no helpmeets for them ;
Donald has got certainly what
    He in the hag did condemn !
His are the crutches and wrinkles,
    His just as surely as hers ;
Peggy would quiz wooing of his,
    She a young lover prefers.

" Up in the Highlands of Scotland,
    Pride goes in front of a fall,

Womankind rules, mankind are fools,
  Girls are the nicest of all!
Mists hang their wreaths on the moun-
    tains;
  Heaths on the moorlands are fair.
Up in the Highlands of Scotland
  Life is the same as elsewhere!"

December, 1867.

Books for the Young

PUBLISHED BY

STRAHAN AND COMPANY.
3 MH 68

STORIES TOLD TO A CHILD.
By the Author of 'Studies for Stories.'
With Illustrations by HOUGHTON, LAWSON, and
ELTZE.
32mo, cloth, gilt, 3s. 6d.

THE GOLD THREAD.
A STORY FOR THE YOUNG.
BY NORMAN MACLEOD, D.D.
With Illustrations by J. D. WATSON, GOURLAY
STEELL, and J. MACWHIRTER.
Cloth, gilt extra, 3s. 6d.

THE MAGIC MIRROR.
A ROUND OF TALES FOR OLD AND YOUNG.
BY WILLIAM GILBERT.
With Illustrations by W. S. GILBERT.
Crown 8vo, 5s.

THE POSTMAN'S BAG.
A Story Book for Boys and Girls.
By JOHN DE LIEFDE.
With Illustrations by J. Pettie, R. Bell, and others.
Crown 8vo, 3s. 6d.

WORDSWORTH'S POEMS FOR THE YOUNG
With Illustrations by J. Pettie and J. Mac-Whirter.
Square 8vo, 3s. 6d.

DEALINGS WITH THE FAIRIES.
By GEORGE MACDONALD.
With Illustrations by Arthur Hughes.
32mo, cloth, gilt, 2s. 6d.

LILLIPUT LEVEE.
Poems of Childhood, Child-Fancy, and Childlike Moods.
With Illustrations by J. E. Millais, G. J. Pinwell and others.
32mo, cloth, gilt, 2s. 6d.

"THE WILL-O'-THE-WISPS ARE IN TOWN."
AND OTHER TALES.
BY HANS CHRISTIAN ANDERSEN.

With Illustrations by M. E. EDWARDS, ELTZE, and others.

32mo, cloth, gilt, 2s. 6d.

THE WASHERWOMAN'S FOUNDLING.
BY WILLIAM GILBERT.

With Illustrations by W. SMALL.

32mo, cloth, gilt, 2s. 6d.

EDWIN'S FAIRING.
BY EDWARD MONRO, M.A.

With Illustrations by W. JONES.

32mo, cloth, gilt, 2s. 6d.

ÆSOP'S FABLES.
A NEW EDITION.

With 100 Illustrations by WOLF, ZWECKER, and DALZIEL.

32mo, cloth, gilt, 2s. 6d.

STORIES TOLD TO A CHILD.

With Illustrations by HOUGHTON, LAWSON, and ELTZE.

In 32mo, cloth, gilt, 6d. each.

I.

THE GRANDMOTHER'S SHOE.

II.

THE GOLDEN OPPORTUNITY.

III.

THE SUSPICIOUS JACKDAW, AND MR. JOHN SMITH.

IV.

THE MOORISH GOLD, AND THE ONE-EYED SERVANT.

V.

LITTLE RIE AND THE ROSEBUDS, AND CAN AND COULD.

VI.

DEBORAH'S BOOK, AND THE LONELY ROCK.

VII.

THE MINNOWS WITH THE SILVER TAILS, AND TWO WAYS OF TELLING A STORY.

VIII.

THE WILD DUCK SHOOTER, AND I HAVE A RIGHT.

POEMS WRITTEN FOR A CHILD.

By TWO FRIENDS.

With Illustrations.

32mo, cloth, gilt, 3*s*. 6*d*.

DAILY DEVOTIONS FOR CHILDREN.

By MRS. G. HINSDALE.

32mo, 1*s*. 6*d*.

DAILY MEDITATIONS FOR CHILDREN.

By MRS. G. HINSDALE.

32mo, 1*s*. 6*d*.

STRAHAN AND CO., 56, LUDGATE HILL.